CW01509234

ADVANCE PRAISE FOR *THE HEART OF A CHEETAH*

◇◇◇◇◇◇◇◇◇◇◇◇◇◇◇◇

"A raw, unapologetic, and inspiring book about the way Africans can finally achieve widespread economic prosperity."

—**EFOSA OJOMO**, co-author of *The Prosperity Paradox: How Innovation Can Lift Nations Out of Poverty* and current leader of the Global Prosperity research group at the Clayton Christensen Institute for Disruptive Innovation

"*Cheetah* is a truthful portrayal holding wisdom for upcoming African entrepreneurs. Magatte's life and journey are proof that a global brand from humble beginnings is possible. *Cheetah* offers incredible insight into one entrepreneur's mind, reminding us that there are many paths to prosperity, not one prescriptive journey."

—**WILLIAM KAMKWAMBA**, author, *The Boy Who Harnessed the Wind*

"Africans are poor because they are not allowed to create companies due to the layers and layers of powerful government bureaucracies that interfere at every point. Government has stifled the creative spirit of entrepreneurship at every point, which as Magatte points out, is profoundly un-African. Through Magatte's story, we see a strong spirit confronting terrific challenges and failures in creating her business and products."

—**CANDACE SMITH**, author of "The Entrepreneur as Hero," and **VERNON SMITH**, 2002 Nobel Laureate in Economics

"Magatte Wade's is the most compelling voice I know connecting Conscious Capitalism with Africa. The Black Panther is a fictional superhero. *Cheetahs* are real."

-DAVID GARDNER, Chief Rule Breaker, The Motley Fool

"Magatte Wade truly has *The Heart of a Cheetah*—her passion, commitment to entrepreneurship and freedom, love of Africa, and her burning desire to do good in our world shines forth on every page of this book. Her fascinating life story begins in a poor village in Senegal where she was born and initially raised by her grandmother. Still a young girl she immigrates first to Germany to be reunited with her parents and younger sisters and then to France two years later. She studies business in France and at age 20 she decides to move to the United States, where she would be both independent from her parents and would have more opportunities to create her own life path. The move to the United States opened up many opportunities for Magatte, but most importantly was her entrepreneurial passion to create her own business. This she has successfully done more than once and learned many invaluable lessons about business, life, and people. She is not afraid or ashamed to admit her mistakes, which I believe is one of the keys to success in both business and life. Magatte's story is one of continuous personal growth. She rapidly becomes disillusioned by the false promises that socialism makes about prosperity and equality. She comes to understand that economic freedom, entrepreneurship, and lessening oppressive government regulations, tariffs, and taxes are the key to prosperity both for individuals and for countries. This is the vision Magatte has for helping Africa to create the prosperity and dignity that will help its 1.2 billion people to fully flourish in the 21st century."

-JOHN MACKEY, CEO & Co-Founder, Whole Foods Market

"In this disarmingly frank and compelling book Magatte Wade tells the story of her life and why, haunted by the struggles of her fellow Africans, she has devoted it to their betterment and ending that complex of inferiority that is Africa. It deserves to be a bestseller, to do better than Rachel Carson's *Silent Spring*, to genuinely change the beliefs and understanding on the subject of wealth creation and why it is so difficult in Africa."

-LINDA WHETSTONE, former Chairman of Atlas Network and Past President of the Mont Pelerin Society.

"After reading this book, I sat in silence for hours. With a heart full of both pride and pain. I began to visualize thousands of *Cheetahs* in unison running faster and faster — jumping over every obstacle that tried to slow them down. Unstoppable, with one goal and one dream ... to lift up and make prosperous again our motherland, AFRICA!

Africa shall rise up again because the hearts of the *Cheetahs* are now beating as one!

Magatte has inspired me to run with the *Cheetahs*!"

-ALICE MARIE JOHNSON, Relentless Criminal Justice Reform Advocate, former prisoner, author of *After Life: My Journey from Incarceration to Freedom,* and United Nation "Women's Rights Defender."

"As revealed in *The Heart of a Cheetah*, Magatte Wade is a force of nature who speaks some uncomfortable truths to well-intentioned people. The core of that uncomfortable truth is that some people love the poor so much they create systems that insure there will be many more of them to love. Her message must be heard by anyone who honestly wants to be part of the solution."

-FR. ROBERT SIRICO, author of *The Economics of the Parables* and President Emeritus of the Acton Institute

"Magatte Wade is possibly the most beautiful person I have ever met — not only is she stunningly beautiful on the outside, she has an incredible heart that is both sensitive and tough at the same time. If you have the privilege to read *The Heart of a Cheetah*, you will begin to understand what makes her such an incredible person who cares so deeply for the people of the world in which we all live. You will be humbled, inspired and hopefully motivated to act. I am a strong believer that capitalism can be a force for good and as Chapter 13 is so aptly titled 'There is no end to solutions,' we can all become part of the solution."

–GLORIA NELUND, Founder and CEO of TriLinc Global

"You. Must. Read. This. Book.

Magatte Wade is a member of the *Cheetah Generation*. She speaks words that crack open the general global understanding of Africa, and releases 'Lightning out of the Bottle.' *What is this lightning?* Believe you can, then do it. The timeless marketplace, the common law systems which operated for hundreds of years in Africa provide deep foundations for a thrilling thriving future. I grew up in Singapore, I lived through the change she speaks of. Singapore took no aid, instead the people took the action needed, and found pride in themselves. Singapore's bootstrap was a model for China's economic miracle. There is nothing more powerful than believing in yourself. Magatte makes clear from many compelling personal narratives: Never giving up is the secret ingredient."

-MEI LIN FUNG, Chair of: People Centered Internet, co-founded with Vint Cerf, IEEE Technical Committee on Sustainability, SSIT, IEEE Assessment Humanitarian Activities Committee, IEEE Standards Association IC Social Impact Measurement

"To say that Magatte Wade wears her heart on her sleeve is an understatement. Magatte is on a mission to do what very few entrepreneurs, academics, or even political leaders have been able to do: to truly explain the causes of poverty in Africa and get people in her beloved Senegal and across Africa out of poverty, one job at a time. In this powerful book Magatte masterfully takes us on a journey between her personal story, the practical and uplifting nature of entrepreneurship, and an analysis of policy issues in a simple but nuanced manner. The *Cheetah Generation* will be all the better by following this road map Magatte has drawn, and we should heed her call and example and empower the *Cheetah Generation* to get Africa back on the path to fulfill its full potential and secure human flourishing for all Africans."

-GONZALO SCHWARZ, CEO, Archbridge Institute

"A manifesto for liberation.

To much of the world, poverty in Africa is assumed to be natural and inevitable. Now comes Magatte Wade with a powerful message that it is neither. From personal experience, she knows that Africans are as entrepreneurial as any people. We can find man-made obstacles to progress, rooted in bad ideas and bad character, on every continent. Because Magatte Wade overcame them herself, and understands the liberating principles of freedom and free markets, her book will now inspire and transform not only impressions of Africa but Africa itself."

-LAWRENCE W. REED, President Emeritus, Foundation for Economic Education.

"There have been books worth reading on the need to unleash free market capitalism in poor countries as the only way to end global poverty. Senegalese-born entrepreneur Magatte Wade writes with a passion and urgency that brings this important idea to a new level. *The Heart of a Cheetah* is a very special book that can truly change minds and hearts."

—**GENE EPSTEIN,** Director of the Soho Forum, former economics editor, Barron's

"For decades, most of sub-Saharan Africa was considered a lost cause. The most common phrase written was 'a never-ending cycle of poverty.' NGO's and governments spent billions, to little avail. Yet the people of Africa have tremendous desire and energy to rise up to global living standards. Here, in *The Heart of a Cheetah*, Senegalese-American entrepreneur and thinker Magatte Wade offers a solution: freedom. Filled with compelling stories and brilliant wisdom from the people, this wonderful book gives us all a whole new perspective on Africa, Africans, and their challenges and opportunities."

—**GARY HOOVER,** Executive Director, American Business History Center

"Magatte Wade forcefully rejects the virtue-signaling paternalism of so many who want to 'lift up' African nations that struggle with poverty. Instead, she shows that Africans will lift themselves up, thank you — and their progress would be faster if the institutions of free enterprise were better protected in their countries. Bursting with personality and passion, *The Heart of a Cheetah* tours the ups and downs of Magatte's career as a serial entrepreneur and thought leader, and, from these experiences, draws important lessons that point the way for a brighter future in Africa."

—**BRAD LIPS,** CEO, Atlas Network

"When she was a child, Magatte Wade established social order by identifying and punching bullies in the face. In her engaging page-turner *The Heart of a Cheetah*, Magatte uses her mighty pen to analyze private sector and philanthropic bullies and their mandates, which have enforced centuries of demeaning African 'helpless' stereotypes and counterproductive economic policies. She details the clogged bureaucracies that delay financial independence across the African continent, using history as a backdrop. Taking sharp aim at poverty porn leadership, Magatte successfully demonstrates that respect for African cultures and well-meaning 'charity' has resulted in zero return on investment. Her work also illustrates how aid campaigns have enforced an inferiority complex in the souls of millions of Africans. These ill-informed rescue missions strip all Africans of their innate dignity and desire to liberate themselves. With heartwarming candor, Magatte candidly and courageously shares her personal and entrepreneurial challenges and victories. Instead of a treatise of grievances, Magatte eloquently provides scalable action plans for Africa. *The Heart of a Cheetah* should be studied by the private sector, at universities and implemented throughout the African Diaspora."

-SABRINA LAMB, Founder/CEO, Wekeza.com and WorldofMoney.org

"In 2007, French president Sarkozy said that the African man has not gone down in history enough. Magatte demonstrates here in a unique and unprecedented way that not only is Africa at the heart of the economic history of the world but that in addition African civilizations too long denigrated and forgotten, sometimes by Africans themselves, have the solutions to answer to the challenges of the next 30 years. *The Heart of a Cheetah* is a necessary and vital book to read for anyone truly committed to peace, democracy, social and climate justice not only for Africans but also for the world."

"Magatte Wade has written a very moving and informative memoir of an African entrepreneur's tireless efforts to produce high-quality goods in Africa for the world market. The goal of Magatte's efforts has been to demonstrate that Africans are quite capable of lifting themselves out of poverty, if not prevented from doing so by government-created obstacles."

THE HEART
OF A
CHEETAH

How We Have Been Lied to about African Poverty,
and What That Means for Human Flourishing

BY MAGATTE WADE

CHEETAH
PRESS

The Heart of A Cheetah,
Magatte Wade

ISBN Hardcover: 979-8-218-27667-6
ISBN Paperback: 979-8-9892027-0-6
ISBN Ebook: 979-8-9892027-1-3
ISBN Audiobook: 979-8-9892027-2-0

Magatte@MagatteWade.com
MagatteWade.com
Printed in the USA

DEDICATION

To Ibrahima Ndour and my beloved
Professor George Ayittey

TABLE OF CONTENTS

FOREWORD BY GEORGE AYITTEY

◇◇◇◇◇◇◇◇◇◇◇◇◇◇

T HERE IS HOPE FOR AFRICA, and it rests with the *Cheetah Generation.* I coined the expression out of an oddball experience. In one's work, certain experiences may come as innocent, everyday, run-of-the-mill events but have a profound import. One such memorable experience occurred to me in July 2003, when I was writing the book *Africa Unchained.* I was invited to Ghana by Dr. Charles Mensa, executive director of the Institute of Economic Affairs, to participate in a three-day workshop at Elmina. My task was to give a series of lectures on globalization and rent-seeking activities to a group of young African graduates. There were about thirty of them from Nigeria, Ivory Coast, Senegal, Sierra Leone, and, of course, Ghana.

These young African graduates were quite energetic and intellectually astute. What made my day at the workshop was a young Sierra Leonean called Mustapha—about twenty-four years old. He had told his friends he was going to take part in a workshop in Ghana. Thereupon, they had asked him who the speakers were to be. When he mentioned Professor Ayittey, his friends became "ecstatic" (his own words) and demanded "proof" that I would indeed be speaking. They insisted that Mustapha record every word I said.

Upon arriving in Ghana, Mustapha went to town and purchased a small tape recorder to record my lectures, but he lost it just before he got to the workshop. Rats! Thinking that he would be in "big trouble" (his words) if he returned to Sierra Leone without the tape, he rushed back to town and scrounged for hours before finding another tape recorder to purchase. By the time he got back, my lectures were over. Poor guy! To save his neck, he got me to repeat "I am Professor George Ayittey" over and over into the tape recorder. I also gave him copies of my lectures.

I may have saved his neck, but he left a deep impression on me. In my interactions with Mustapha and his friends, I discovered that they come from a new generation of young African graduates and professionals. These young adults look at African issues and problems from a totally unique perspective. They may be classified as the Cheetah Generation—Africa's new hope. They do not relate to the old colonialist paradigm, to the slave trade, or to Africa's postcolonial nationalist leaders such as Kwame Nkrumah, Jomo Kenyatta, Kenneth Kaunda, or Julius Nyerere. The Cheetahs know that many of their current leaders are hopelessly corrupt, that their governments are ridiculously rotten and, further, they commit flagitious human rights violations. They brook no nonsense about corruption, inefficiency, ineptitude, incompetence, or buffoonery. They understand and stress transparency, accountability, human rights, and good governance. They do not have the stomach for colonial-era politics. In fact, they were not even born in that era. As such, they do not make excuses for or seek to explain away government failures in terms of colonialism and the slave trade. Unencumbered by the old shibboleths of colonialism, imperialism, and other external adversities, they can analyze issues with remarkable clarity and objectivity.

Their outlook and perspectives are totally different from many African leaders, intellectuals, and elites, whose mental faculties are so foggy and their reasoning or logic so befuddled they cannot distinguish between right and wrong. They see a Western imperialist plot in every African adversity and have rallied to the defense of such African leaders as Robert Mugabe of Zimbabwe simply because he fought against colonial rule. Having liberated their countries, such leaders were transformed into demigods who could do no wrong. This is the Hippo Generation—intellectually astigmatized and stuck in their colonialist pedagogical patch. They can see with eagle-eyed clarity the injustices perpetrated by Whites against Blacks, but they are hopelessly blind to the more heinous injustices perpetrated—right under their very noses—by the Mugabes, the Ghaddafis, the Eyademas, the Obiangs, and others. The Hippos only see oppression and exploitation when perpetrated by Westerners or White people. The Cheetahs are not so intellectually astigmatized.

I told these young Africans to take the Cheetah Pledge—that is, they must seek their wealth in the private sector. More importantly, they should shun the government sector. The reasons are twofold: first, government has been the source of many of Africa's problems. Second, it can be dangerous. If you are working in a government department where everybody is stealing, it will be difficult to remain clean. Eventually, you will be suspected of being a snitch. They may besmirch your reputation and find ways of implicating you in a scandal.

After the workshop I went on to popularize the Cheetah concept in my TED Conference speech in Arusha in July 2007. I identified and wrote about a few Cheetahs in my recent books. Cheetahs are problem solvers and entrepreneurs. They are not going to sit there and wait for governments to come and solve problems for them. Having written about them, it was my earnest wish to have a Cheetah write their own story, detailing how they got started, what obstacles they came up against, and how they overcame them. Most importantly, I wanted them to provide any suggestions they might care to offer to the younger generation. I cannot write this for them.

My prayers were answered when Magatte Wade came up with her book, *The Heart of a Cheetah*. It is a godsend and fits the bill to a T. You can imagine my elation as I browsed through it. This is precisely the book I was looking for. It is essential that it be read by policymakers and students alike. It symbolizes the throbbing energy, power, and rhythm of an African entrepreneur.

Magatte's life story is as remarkable as she is. It shatters the mythology of African inferiority that has encased Africa for centuries—a persistent myth that Africa has lacked entrepreneurs. Nothing could be further from the truth. There were free markets, free enterprise, and free trade in Africa before the colonialists stepped foot on the continent. Market activity has been dominated by women. A little secret about the struggle for independence: it was financed through the profits of Africa's market women. Thus, entrepreneurship can be found in Magatte's DNA, so to speak. But she was not born with a silver spoon in her mouth.

Magatte was born in the small, impoverished village of M'Bour. When she was little, her parents left her in the care of her grandmother and emigrated to France. At the age of seven, she joined her parents in Germany for education.

By the time she turned thirty years old, she had established Adina World Beverages—an African-inspired specialty beverage company with more than $30 million in capital and a nationwide distribution in the United States. She has another company in Africa, SkinIsSkin, which produces skin care products with Senegalese recipes. Magatte's book is a remarkable tale of personal triumph in the face of daunting obstacles.

There is a second story, however, beyond just her entrepreneurial ventures, that reflects her intellectual inquisitiveness. She had always wondered why some nations are rich while others are poor. After thirty years of studying the problem assiduously, she found the answer—one that turns the entire development orthodoxy on its head. Over $3 trillion has been pumped into Africa with little to show for it. Magatte advances three reasons Africa remains poor: government overregulation, rampant corruption, and Western charitable efforts that ensnare the population in dependency and destroy productive programs.

She believes the solution lies in opening up markets, which would get the government out of the way and lead to the reawakening of the entrepreneurial spirit—"the heart of a Cheetah"—that long made Africa a center of fine craftsmanship and free trade.

It is a very simple solution. It makes you wonder why no one has thought of it previously.

This book should have been written a long time ago. It would have provided Africa with the truly indigenous and successful route to prosperity. I have always stated that Africa's salvation does not lie inside the corridors of the World Bank, the IMF, or the US Congress. Neither does it lie in the inner sanctum of the Chinese Politburo.

Africa's salvation rests on the backs of the Cheetah Generation. This is their guidebook, and it has my fullest endorsement.

—GEORGE B. N. AYITTEY, PhD, Washington, DC
November 3, 2020

LETTER FROM MAGATTE

◇◇◇◇◇◇◇◇◇◇◇◇◇

WHY IS AFRICA STILL POOR?
It's a question that I get asked a lot, and it's haunted me for years. It haunts me because the answer is so simple, yet everyone still misses it.

You might believe it's due to colonization. Certainly colonization was often horrifically cruel and left many scars.

But (and I know this will anger many) I do not believe colonization is the root cause of poverty in Africa today, more than sixty years afterward. Many countries have been colonized, yet they've risen out of poverty.

Look at Singapore. Look at Dubai. Look at South Korea. Even China. These countries were all poor, until one day, they were not.

Mauritius, a tiny African island with almost no economic activity in 1960, is now in the top third globally. Botswana is an upper middle-income country. Rwanda has been growing at a rapid clip in recent years.

So what is the answer? Why are so many African nations still poor while a few are rising?

Is it corruption? Geography? Education? Skills? Malnutrition?

If you're not an entrepreneur, then the answer is invisible to you. You fail to see it because you likely come from a country where you take it for granted. You probably never have to think about it.

The answer: Africa's business environments are the worst in the world.

It's because of our laws that Africa's business owners are in chains. These chains hold us back from ever creating wealth or running thriving businesses.

In Singapore, Denmark, New Zealand, or the United States, it is fairly simple to start a business. By contrast, in most African nations, it is really difficult. The laws that make it possible to do business in Africa are literally among the worst in the world.

You can look it up for yourself. Of the twenty lowest-ranked countries in the world for starting a business, Africa makes up thirteen of them. That's nearly 70 percent!

There is only one way for Africa to become prosperous, and it's not through charity, aid, or education. It's through businesses.

Businesses create jobs. Jobs pay people money. And when Africans have money, they will no longer be poor.

Simple equation, right?

Unfortunately, no.

We will stay stuck in an endless cycle of poverty until these chains are finally broken and our markets are set free.

Perhaps you're wondering why this matters to you. Maybe you're not African, and your life is just fine. Why should you care?

Because by 2050, 25 percent of the world's population will be African. That's right: one out of every four people walking this Earth will be African.

And do you know what the average age is in Africa? Nineteen years old!

In North America and Europe, that number is thirty-eight and forty-two years old, respectively.

The future is African. Your fate, and everyone else's, is tied to ours.

As an African entrepreneur myself, I've experienced firsthand the difficulties of doing business in Africa. The infrastructure is a mess; the regulations are absurd, and the bureaucracy is overwhelming. It's nearly impossible to start formal/legal companies, hire employees, and grow.

But there is hope. There is a path forward.

The path to prosperity in Africa is through Startup Cities. These are cities with their own law and governance that are designed to provide a friendly and enabling environment where businesses can take hold and thrive, creating jobs and opportunities for everyone.

It's not a fantasy; it's a proven strategy. Countries all over the world have followed similar models that empower entrepreneurs and innovation. The result is always the same: wealth and prosperity for the citizens of those countries.

Startup Cities hold the power to break the chains of poverty in Africa. The creation of world-class business environments is the proven path to our prosperous future.

◇◇◇◇◇◇◇◇◇◇◇◇◇◇◇

When I first set out to write this book, I wanted to create something that would be of value to anyone who is passionate about making a positive impact in Africa. Whether you are African or not, living in Africa or not, an activist, an investor, a donor, or an entrepreneur, I believe there is something in this book for you.

One thing I can promise you is that this book is not a feel-good story about charity and aid. It is a story about the realities of doing business in Africa and the unique challenges that entrepreneurs face in this region. It is a story about why every outside attempt to "save poor Africa" has failed and will continue to fail. But most of all, it is a story about Africa's potential to be a beacon of hope for the world.

As an African woman who was born in Senegal, grew up in France, built a successful career in Silicon Valley, and then created profitable businesses in both Africa and the United States, I am uniquely qualified to guide you through this journey.

When I was thirty years old, I'd founded an African-inspired beverage company called Adina, with more than $30 million in capital and nationwide distribution in the United States. I currently run another business in Africa called SkinIsSkin, which produces skin care products with Senegalese recipes.

I've also had the blessing of speaking all over the world on this topic: at the United Nations, TED, the Aspen Institute, Harvard, Yale, MIT, Stanford, and the Clinton Global Initiative, as well as conferences in France, the UK, Dubai, Guatemala, Nigeria, Saudi Arabia, Rwanda, Gabon, Senegal, Tanzania, Mauritania, and more.

And I'd imagine some of you may have heard my ideas on Jordan Peterson's podcast or Lex Fridman's podcast, which—at the time of this writing—collectively have more than ten million views.

So as you hold this book in your hands, I want to thank you for taking the time to read my story. I am passionate about sharing my knowledge and experience with others, and it's my life's mission to create prosperity in my beloved Africa.

I invite you to read this book with an open mind and an open heart as you walk a mile in the shoes of an African entrepreneur. It is my hope that by doing so, your beliefs about helping Africa will change from "poverty reduction" to prosperity building.

As a token of my gratitude, I'm giving you a free copy of the audiobook. Enjoy!

SCAN THE QR CODE TO INSTANTLY DOWNLOAD
YOUR FREE AUDIOBOOK.

It's time to stop looking down on Africans. It's time to stop the endless cycle of charity and aid that only leads to more poverty.

It's time to invest in African businesses and provide the environments and resources we need to thrive. The key lies in Startup Cities, which will unleash the potential of Africa and its people.

Join me in this mission. Together, we can create a bright future for Africa and a better world for everyone.

CHAPTER ONE

Ku ëmb sa sanqal, ëmb sa kersa. (He who keeps in a
sack the millet flour that feeds you keeps in the
same sack your dignity.)

◇◇◇◇◇◇◇◇◇◇◇◇◇

LISTEN AND I WILL TELL YOU A STORY.
This isn't the story of my life. That will come later.
This story concerns words. Words that I never thought
I would hear said to me by another human being. They were
said to me by a young Senegalese woman I'd hired to work in
my factory. You must understand. I love these young ladies who
work in my factory. They have thrown their hearts into jobs that
are quite different from what they are used to. They were raised
and trained to cook and clean, but now they are creating products as fine as any found in the world. They are doing this in an
African factory—my factory.

They are my heroes.

That morning the young woman, Nafi, basically said to me,
about us—us Africans, "Maybe we are inferior."

Her words shattered my heart. I needed to hear these words,
though, because I was—and still am—haunted. What haunts me
is story after story of my people, my fellow Senegalese, who now
lie at the bottom of the ocean.

They are fish food.

They are fish food because few in this world are focused on real solutions for Africa. Very few are focused on the essential need to create jobs.

But those at the bottom of the ocean were my people—people who looked just like me. And they were—many of them—so young!

Do you really think that's the best we can do—to serve as fish food?

They were trying to make their way to Europe, so they climbed into boats that were too small and too crowded, not at all adequate for this type of sea crossing. They were desperate for jobs.

I've heard these stories all my life.

And then there were stories about bodies that fell out of airplanes: the bodies of people hiding in the landing gear of the plane. Some hid in the baggage compartment and froze to death.

And there were others, too, who decided to go overland through Libya. Do you know what happens to us when we cross through Libya and are caught?

We are sold as slaves. For $500. Sometimes $300.

Wouldn't you be haunted if you were like me, and you heard these stories from the time you were a little girl, and you heard them over and over? Wouldn't you be haunted?

That morning—the morning I heard the woman's words wondering if we were inferior—I admit I was anxious. I had decided to gather my team in Senegal to finally explain to them who I truly am and what makes me do what I do.

We were to gather at the factory, which is in Mékhé, a small town a little more than one hundred miles from Dakar, the capital of Senegal. Mékhé is poor, and from that standpoint it resembles many small villages in many developing countries in the world. Mostly it consists of concrete block buildings, most covered with a coat of dust from the dirt streets. Many are homes to small family businesses selling sodas and snack food. Some function as restaurants. Anything to make a CFA (a "buck"—Communauté financière Africaine).

Mékhé is not necessarily beautiful by any means. But the people who live there love it, in the mysterious way all people love their homes. I love it.

That morning I joined the goats and horse carts on the street. People were busily moving about, stepping around the piles of horse manure in the deep powdery dirt that makes up our streets. It was already hot.

This meeting was important to me because we had reached several crucial milestones: the employees were now properly trained, and we had successfully conducted our first round of sample batch production. In a few days, I would be in America, our target market for these African-made products and also my husband's home.

I was exhausted. This was the tail end of a year of relentless travel, with at least six transatlantic flights, plus many flights within North America and Africa. Starting and running a business anywhere is difficult. In Africa, it is even more challenging.

I could say I built the factory, but it's perhaps more accurate to say I assembled it—an often crazy task given both the lack of proper lab equipment and supplies in Senegal and the difficulty and expense of importing them.

But that was just the start. I also conducted the research and development on the product formulation. Because I was determined to use African resources, I often had to seek and find suppliers and create relationships. These relationships were often difficult because my quality standards requirements were rarely available from local suppliers. And I was charged a 45 percent tariff on every item I imported—a tariff that makes importing supplies into Senegal often prohibitive for small companies like mine.

Consider, for example, the struggles I faced to get cardboard boxes for packaging my products in Senegal. In Senegal, there are only two manufacturers of cardboard boxes. The quality is not ideal. In order to get new boxes, I needed to order at least one thousand pieces of any given size and shape. We needed two box sizes: one in which to pack the bulk lip balms and another one to hold those smaller boxes so they could be shipped. That meant I needed to order two thousand boxes (one thousand boxes of each size). When I got started I only needed fifty boxes of each.

The process takes four to eight weeks for the first order of custom boxes after the customer approves the samples—a process that can take several weeks. If I have too much inventory of empty boxes I have to store them, and unless the storage is in a warehouse that keeps bugs and dust out, they become unusable after a few weeks. I had to pay 50 percent of the order upfront. It often took a long time to explain what I wanted to ensure that I got the right box. Rather than continuing to order custom boxes, I was eventually able to find another business that had excess quantities of a box that was close enough—not quite the right size and quality, but okay as a stopgap measure.

That is what I need to do to get cardboard boxes in Senegal. Again, if I import them from the outside world, I'm charged a 45 percent tariff, making it too expensive.

By contrast, in the United States I can get exactly the boxes I need for less than $100 using my credit card. If I order what I want before 6:00 p.m., I can get it delivered to my US facility the next day.

This anecdote is not just about boxes. Most items needed for a business are expensive and inordinately difficult to source in Senegal. Does your business have a printer, photocopier, and computer? In Senegal all office equipment is roughly 50 percent or more expensive than it is in the United States, with far fewer options.

Why don't we have enough jobs in Senegal? Why are our young people crossing the Atlantic in tiny fishing boats in an attempt to get to Europe, with dreams of a better life?

Because it is like swimming through molasses to start a manufacturing business in Senegal—the kind of manufacturing business that creates jobs.

Putting together my factory was just one of the difficulties I faced. Some were more personal. There was, for example, the extended stress of pouring money into a product that I knew would require the breaking down of many prejudices.

I knew that while most people do not mind buying clothes, jewelry, and other nonconsumable goods made in Africa, many people would reject African products that, in the US, require regulatory oversight, including hygiene licenses for the factory and extensive labeling requirements.

Yes, there are products that claim to be African, or at least are Africa-inspired. At best, they use some African ingredients. It is rare to have cosmetic products actually manufactured in Africa (except maybe South Africa) and exported to Europe or the United States. But I had decided to have my factory in Senegal, even though I knew the initial response would be wary at best.

Because I knew that would be the case, I had been very hard on myself and the team. We were to be extra careful about everything. I stressed over the details. We were all tired, I think. And excited. And nervous.

I had decided that I would start the day with a general meeting. That morning when they arrived, Ibrahima, my team leader, told the ladies that we would be convening in the main production room because I wanted to talk to them. After the usual preparation protocol, including handwashing, hand sanitizing, and changing into lab coats, lab shoes, and hairnets, we all went to the table. We prepared a beautiful tray with coffee, milk, sugar, and mugs and then chose our seats.

It was not yet 11:00 a.m., but the temperature outside was already 95 degrees Fahrenheit. Inside, thanks to air conditioning, we were enjoying a cool 77 degrees Fahrenheit, as required for our manufacturing process. For a few minutes we were cracking jokes with each other while preparing our coffee and tea. Once everyone had what they needed, they were silent. I could tell they had no idea what I wanted to talk about. But on this important day, I did have something to say. I would finally share with them the reason behind all of this.

I took a deep breath and spoke to the group:

"I will tell you what drives me and what made me come to this small village to set up my business."

"It's just because you are such a good person, Magatte," inserted Mame Marème.

Mame Marème. So many times I had been on the verge of letting her go because at first she was struggling with timeliness, and she lacked a sense of initiative in her work. After a few frustrating episodes, Ibrahima (I called him Ibou) asked me to please take a step back and let him nurture her skills. He knew exactly what I needed to hear.

"Your eagerness and the weight you carry make you impatient," he said to me. "None of them has ever had an official job, let alone one of this nature. You came to a small village here in rural Senegal, bringing the highest standards in the world to employees who never had a job in their lives. Yes, each one of these women has always worked, caring for her home and family. They do so with great bravery and dignity. But this is all new for them.

"And I know you. I know your heart. I know that is precisely the reason you are doing this: to give them a chance at something else beyond household work. But this is not the way you will motivate anyone. Even me, your friend of the past ten years, I have had to press my heart many times since we started working together. I know you feel stressed, but you can't do this. You can't put it on us like this. Let me work with the team. We will all get there. Each one of us will get to that world-class level you talk about, and beyond. But for that, you need to refrain from being impatient. Watch the tone of your voice when you speak. Remember that you command and inspire the energy of this place."

And then he told me something that hurt. "Some of these women are so scared of you, and of disappointing you, they actually make mistakes just out of being nervous around you. So please calm down. Try to smile. We may not have the experience right now, but we are not stupid. There is nothing one can't do if one is properly trained and taught."

Those words made me go to my office and cry. I cried and cried and cried. I cried out of guilt. It was so sad for me to realize that despite everything I had done to create a good working environment for the team, I was the greatest source of pain in their work lives.

But these particular words: "We may not have the experience right now, but we are not stupid." These words made me cry with a piercing disappointment in myself because I then realized that I must have internalized the prejudices that most people have about getting work done in Africa by the locals.

I had heard it from everyone, non-Africans working in Senegal, African people in the Diaspora, and even the locals themselves: "You are going to do *what* in a rural African village?!"

A French man who wanted the contract to help set up our lab even told me, "You should make rules around when to use the bathroom; otherwise they will abuse it."

I heard them all, and even though I was determined to prove them wrong, I was growing more anxious with each mistake.

I had forgotten that it is normal to make mistakes, especially while learning something new. I still have not forgiven myself for forgetting that fact. But I listened and heard. And I put my new knowledge to work.

"Thank you, Mame Marème," I replied, smiling. "But it's not because I'm kind. God knows I have been very demanding. I am sure each of you has had moments when you were probably cursing me, particularly at the beginning."

I saw Mame Marème smile discreetly.

And I continued, "I gathered everyone today because we have been working together for months now. I want to tell you why I have pushed you so hard."

Consider who was in that room. Among the employees and besides Ibou, none had been beyond the Senegalese border. Some had never been to Dakar, the capital city. The fact that I, a fellow Senegalese, had lived in France and Germany and the United States made me an exotic creature in their eyes, worthy of respect—surely beyond what I deserved.

I told them some difficult truths.

I told them the world is prejudiced against products "made in Africa." In some ways that wasn't difficult for them to understand because we have this sense of cultural inferiority. Whether conscious or not, whether we admit it or not, for many among us, we tend to think that what comes from us is not good enough. I explained that we were part of a great enterprise to change the perception of Africa. To do that, I said, we needed to be above suspicion. Above prejudice. Simply being good enough was a luxury our African factory couldn't afford. A mistake here, a corner cut there, and we would join the many other African companies that had no brand credibility, especially in the West. I explained that was the reason we had to establish and follow quality control procedures to match any in the world.

Sitting at that table and looking around, my heart was suddenly full of gratitude for each of them and for their dedication to work well done. I gained a new heart. I was filled with hope and new dedication. They had developed more pride in our company than I had, if that were even possible. And I thanked them.

"As you guys know, I am leaving in a few days, and everything we created here will now rest on your shoulders. I will not be here to micromanage you. You also know why your work here matters so much in terms of our credibility in our marketplace in America." They were grave, listening carefully.

I told them I had confidence in their ability to create products that would become well known and respected throughout the world.

"Look at us," I said. "Together we are creating products inspired by the traditions and great wisdom of the people of our country. We're manufacturing in Africa. We're creating new jobs."

I could see the pride in their faces, and I continued.

"We're bringing something new to those in wealthy countries—not just new products but new knowledge. We are showing them their belief that Africa has nothing to contribute to the world is wrong. And we are doing one more thing: we are bringing back the ancient African way of business. For hundreds of years, a millennium or more, Africa was prosperous—as wealthy as any land in the world. In those days we had our own trade routes, no less rich than the Silk Road or the Spice Route. Timbuktu and Aksum were magnificent trade centers.

"But then we lost it all. Now you and I are together rebuilding African prosperity. That's why we don't ask people to provide us with charity: because often charity hurts. And we don't ask them to buy our products to help us."

I picked up a handful of our lip balms and continued. "We want them to buy our products because these?" I said while pointing at the lip balms. "These are special. These are premium, and these are African."

When I finished, I looked at Nafi, who was just twenty-six years old and was holding down her first-ever job. Her black skin looked so fresh and damp and beautiful against her white coat. So young. She looked at me and her eyes were filled with tears. "Thank you, Magatte," she said, and then she spoke these words:

"My whole life I have always seen people like me represented in movies, magazines, and such as a poor, hopeless person other people need to help. So I must confess that by now, I have come to believe that maybe us Black African people must be inferior."

I was floored. Tears started swelling up from the depth of my belly. But then she added, "But that is not the reason I am crying." Then I saw her sitting up more straight in her chair, lifting her head, shoulders down and back, straight back. And she said, "I am crying because now I know that it is not true. I am not inferior. Black Africans…we are not inferior."

Her whole being exuded a huge sense of relief, as if a thousand pounds was just lifted off her chest and shoulders.

I cried for joy. I had just witnessed what it looked like for a human being to regain her dignity.

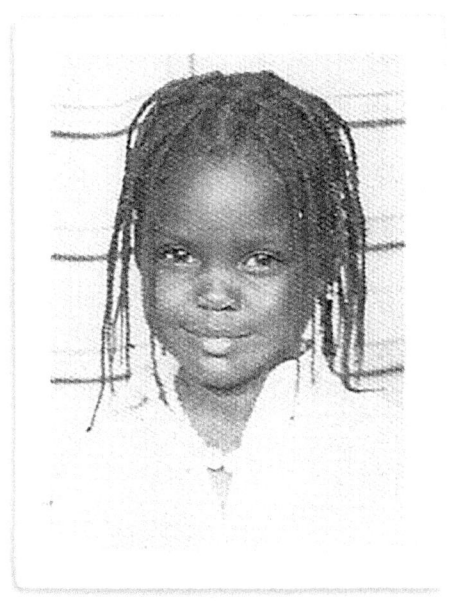

CHAPTER TWO

Ndoxum kese du forox. (Pure water
never turns sour.)

◇◇◇◇◇◇◇◇◇◇◇◇◇◇

I WAS BORN IN AFRICA and spent my first seven years there. I quite often return for work and to reconnect with my people and culture. But I have spent much of my life away, mostly in Europe and the United States. I say this to prove I know what most Westerners think about Africa.

The answer is not much. I mean that in two ways. Yes, there are negative images of Africa. Most Americans, for example, first see in their mind's eye starving Black children, their bellies swollen with hunger. That is the image used by the charities that operate in the West as they seek donations "for the cause." I call that poverty porn.

These images are sometimes interrupted by those of civil wars and campaigns of genocide.

Some people—slightly more enlightened, perhaps—view Africa as a vast Disneyland nature park, with elephants and giraffes striding everywhere across the plains. See *The Lion King*, for example, or *Madagascar*.

Even world maps conspire against Africa, with its Mercator-demanded boundaries diminished to those of Greenland.

Africa is fourteen times larger than Greenland—and 70 percent larger than South America!

The hard truth, however, is that most people in the West don't think about Africa at all.

An unbelievable number of Americans, for example, think "Africa" is a single nation, not fifty-four-plus independent states. I would wager good money that not one American in a hundred could find my native Senegal on a map. Not one in a thousand could identify a picture of Dakar.

Joseph Conrad's novel, written in 1899 at the peak of colonialism, didn't name Africa as *The Heart of Darkness*, but no one has ever doubted that it was Africa that he meant, and was describing. Marlow, the narrator, sought out the undiscovered country, the "blank place" on the map. There he found Black people who were either cannibals or gibbering discarded natives starving on a river bank. Eventually he found Kurtz, the White man everyone described as remarkable. A genius, they said. This same Kurtz had impaled the heads of his Black enemies on poles that encircled his home.

African novelist Chinua Achebe described the impact this book had on him. He pointed out that Conrad didn't bother to confer the power of speech on the natives. Instead, Conrad said they engaged in a "violent babble." Only twice, Achebe said, do natives speak intelligibly. In one instance, the headman of the crew manning Marlow's boat asks Marlow to capture a native who had engaged them in a fight:

> "Catch 'im," he said. "Give 'im to us."
> "To you, eh? What would you do with him?"
> "Eat 'im," says the man.

The most famous books about Africa all have one thing in common. They are about White people—either White colonists or visitors: *Cry, the Beloved Country. Out of Africa. The Power of One.*

Google "movies set in Africa," and a half dozen Tarzan movies pop up.

It's true that Africa has a growing list of fine Black authors, arguably led by Achebe. But none has finally torn open the white veil that surrounds the continent in popular and high culture.

Perhaps the worst offenders are the news media. In their supposed compassion, they have rendered for the world an image of sub-Saharan Africa as a land of eternal violence, poverty, and neglect.

African Americans, as American Blacks call themselves, are also unfamiliar with Africa. In an interview with Al Jazeera, Akon, the singer, songwriter, actor, producer, and entrepreneur—and, like me, a Senegalese American—said African Americans are terrified by the thought of going to Africa.

"Even just for knowledge, just to know where they came from, just to get an idea of what that is; there is so much fear instilled in them that they wouldn't even want to go there to visit. You mention Africa, they start shaking."

And so it is. To most of the world, the people of sub-Saharan Africa are largely invisible. Or perhaps worse, we are simply set pieces in a drama that, as Conrad showed, could be placed anywhere that isn't Western.

Let me tell you what my Africa is like.

A typical home in Mékhé and in most of Senegal is called a "concession," though we would say a "compound" in English. The patriarch and matriarch of the family live in a home with their grown children. It can easily be five or six of those grown children. Each of the grown children who is married lives in a room with their children, usually two or three children under age ten. When they have a fourth child, that family "sub-unit" moves out to their own home, where they will then be reproducing the same model. Their children will eventually marry and will bring their wife in, have children, and stay in the concession until it is time to break out on their own.

In each room where the "sub-family" lives, you will usually find a bed with nightstands, an armoire, a TV, and sometimes a fridge—often an old rickety-raggedy fridge that works only painfully. The children sleep on their parents' bed until they are three years old or so, at which point they will sleep on the floor on a mattress put out at night. If the family has less means, they will sleep on a rug.

Most compounds have twenty-five to thirty people living in them, though some are much larger, depending on the number of children the matriarch and patriarch have. In such a compound, the patriarch usually no longer has to provide for *la dépense quotidienne*, the "daily expenditure," because he is older with grown children. Instead the adult children, each head of a sub-family, are in charge of providing the "*la dépense quotidienne*" for the entire community, taking turns for two days in a row, followed by the next one, and so on and so forth. It can vary from 6,000 CFA (approx $12) a day to 12,000 CFA (approximately $24) a day, depending on the means of the family. That money will usually buy 4–6 kg of rice per day, 3–5 kg of fish or protein per day, and 3–5 kg of vegetables per day to feed the whole concession. That will take care of lunch (the biggest, most elaborate meal of the day) and dinner (which is simpler). Each head of a sub-family (who can and wants to) can give his wife more money to make or buy more food, which they will usually eat in the privacy of their room, unless they are able to share with others.

Breakfast usually costs around 1,500 CFA (approximately $3 per sub-family of four to five people) and is the responsibility of the head of the sub-family. It is eaten by the sub-family, not like the big shared bowls at lunch time and dinner time. In the morning a typical average Senegalese family will eat breakfast

French-style: bread, margarine (butter for those who can afford it), and some native Kinkeliba tea or instant Nescafé coffee. Milk is a luxury, so it is used sparingly, often in a powder form, which is more economical and saves better (it doesn't require refrigeration, which not everyone has access to). I have always preferred the more traditional breakfast: a bowl of oatmeal made of local cereals and *sow* (a yummy dairy "sauce").

Most people don't have a microwave or washing machine. Occasionally, a member of the upper class might, though even then they find it cheaper to hire a maid to wash their clothes by hand.

Everybody has a little grill, like a hibachi. That's what most people cook on. A few have a little tank of propane and a camper stove. But most cook on their little charcoal stove, which contributes to the high rate of death from "indoor pollution."

A car? No. Most of the people in Mékhé walk or get around by horse cart or motorcycle taxi. It is possible to rent a seat in a packed car or bus to get to Dakar, but most people rarely make such a trip.

Forget about a guest room. I mean, an extra room? Unless you're some kind of notable, no room goes unused.

We do have TV. Everybody does. TV brings American movies, French movies, everything. And we love Latin American telenovelas! That's because for a long time telenovelas were the cheapest product the TV stations could buy. So we have all the telenovelas from Mexico and India and Brazil. The Senegalese love melodramas. We never miss an episode, even though we don't always understand what the actors are saying. But we're following the plot!

Most of these shows use voice-over. It's funny because the voiceovers are in French. We're "a French-speaking country," but 80 percent don't speak French well. Senegalese often speak Wolof, which is the main indigenous language, plus their own dialect if they have one.

In recent years there have been many new Senegalese soap operas in French and Wolof. They are widely loved, even if our religious leaders question the morality of the plot lines.

TV brings something else too. It brings images that convey that everyone in Mexico, India, Brazil, and the United States is wealthy beyond belief. Is that not what soap operas around the world tend to convey? I remember as a kid going back to Senegal and explaining to my cousin that there were homeless people in France.

I told him, "I don't like to walk in this particular street near my home because it has homeless people. They're so scary and make me sad."

And my cousin was like, "What?! You say there are White people who are so poor they don't have a home?"

And I said, "Yeah."

And he said, "You're lying. You're lying. That can't be true. There are no poor White people!"

I had these arguments over and over again when I was younger. The African stereotype of White people, up until a few years ago, was that they were always prosperous. The default expectation is, "White people are rich."

Growing up in France I knew some middle- and upper-class Black people, but the common stereotype was that Black people lived in the ghettos and were poor.

Stereotypes live in all of us, and they have their repercussions.

◇◇◇◇◇◇◇◇◇◇◇◇◇◇◇◇

WITH IBOU

When Ibou moved to Mékhé from Dakar to manage my factory he brought his wife and five kids, sheep, chickens, and geese. With the salary the company paid him and with the lower cost of living of a small town, he was able to afford a three-bedroom home. In Dakar he and his family lived in a one-room house, with the only bed for the parents. His children slept on mats laid on the floor.

He had worked as a professional landscaper, and later as a night watchman, but Ibou was of very modest means. He was proud that he provided for his family within his means, and his means alone. He was very principled about this and refused to allow me to provide for much beyond his simple needs.

We bought new beds for the kids, with new mattresses with mosquito nets, bed sheets, duvets, duvet covers, and fluffy pillows. It was the first time in their lives that the children had had their own rooms, their own beds, sheets, duvets, or pillows.

Later I'll explain the immense role that Ibou played in my life, including mentor, spiritual guide, friend, family member, and factory manager. But for now, suffice it to say that he was closer to me than anyone else in Senegal. I loved and cared for his children as if they were a part of my family.

◇◇◇◇◇◇◇◇◇◇◇◇◇◇

The jobs of the working adults in the compounds are various and include the wood or metal workers in the informal sector, midlevel public workers, gas pumpers, security guards, policemen, market ladies, farmers, fishermen, traditional communicators, street vendors, and day workers (if you're lucky, that day there's a masonry job or a cart that needs to be unloaded).

Ninety percent of the jobs in Senegal are in the informal sector. People work hard, and often in very hard conditions. Nothing breaks my heart more than witnessing the street vendors dangerously slaloming between moving cars or working the traffic jam and breathing in all the fumes under the hot, dizzying sun.

They are selling anything, from rags to sunglasses to ironing boards—anything you can think of. It's usually merchandise from India or China or Iran. It is always cheap stuff.

You can basically do your grocery shopping while stuck in the traffic jam. Or they'll show up in your neighborhood, carrying their wares on their backs.

Because almost everyone is short on cash, people are always seeking out those who have maybe a little more than they do. They'll go see a friend or family member and see if they can pry out a little.

They literally go and say, "I have this prescription, and see how much it is? And my child is very sick, and I don't know what to do, and can you help me?"

It's a chain. *Everybody* does it, not just the poor. Even the wealthy do it. It may be as much as $10,000, but more often it's $2 to $10. It's like a cascade. Maybe you go to your brother or a friend of a friend, or maybe you have a relative who knows the minister of finance or someone, anyone, with money.

There is no clear concept of a household budget because everyone is always hustling, and everyone owes money, and everyone is owed money. Every day is a matter of getting by as best you can.

I wanted to hire Ibou to run my factory, but that meant asking him to move from Dakar to Mékhé. I was very hesitant because that meant cutting him off from his network of support in Dakar. That was where he could borrow and lend money. Of course, you can send money back and forth, but proximity is a big help because everything is based on relationships. These networks are why African people mostly don't starve to death.

It is true that Africans are incredibly interdependent. We're interdependent out of necessity, especially in these modern days. We are family- and community-oriented. There are expectations of mutual obligation that are heavy.

This orientation toward family and community, based on mutual obligations, is why so many Americans and Europeans (and even early postcolonial African leaders) believed that indigenous Africans were socialists. They re-interpreted the spirit of *Ubuntu*, "I am because we are," as socialism.

But traditional Africans were also solidly pro-market, supported the rule of law, and were firmly in favor of property rights. Jomo Kenyatta, an anti-colonial activist and the first president of independent Kenya, was tremendously frustrated by this misunderstanding by the West:

> The Gikuyu defended their country collectively, and when talking to a stranger they would refer to the country, land, and everything else as "ours," *borori wiito* or *borori wa Gikuyu,* to show the unity among the people. But the fact remained that every inch of the Gikuyu territory had its owner, with the boundary properly fixed and everyone respecting his neighbour's.[1]

---

1 Jomo Kenyatta, *Facing Mount Kenya: The Traditional Life of the Gikuyu.* Secker and Warburg, 1938.

As Robert Frost, the American poet, noted, "Good fences make good neighbors." Unlike the Marxists, who wanted to "abolish property rights," Africans had the good sense to respect property rights.

George Ayittey, the Ghanaian economist (who wrote the foreword to this book and created the concept of the "Cheetah Generation"), speaks eloquently of how central the market experience has always been for African villagers. He has a deep respect for the women who make up the market. He first began to realize how alien to Africa socialism is when he saw the bureaucrats under Ghanaian socialist leader Jerry Rawlings beating women traders who violated price control laws—sometimes even grabbing their babies out of their arms and crushing their skulls. George's own mother had been a trader in the markets. She confirmed that the attempt to control prices in the marketplace was crazy, brutal, and profoundly un-African!

As George has written, when socialism failed to "produce the goods"—that is, result in prosperity—the military leaders believed that socialism had not been applied firmly enough. Thus, the economic failures were blamed on those market women, who were regarded as "profiteers" when they charged higher prices for goods in the marketplace than were authorized by government edict. Rawlings set up strict price control rules, with tribunals for market women who violated the controls. A woman baker in George's family was jailed for three years of hard labor for making an illegal profit of $1.50 on a loaf of bread. This after eons of free market activity in indigenous African markets in which women could charge whatever they liked!

For normal people it is unimaginable that such things could happen. Yet in 2016 you could still read an interview of Ghanaian socialist Nani-Kofi as he described Rawlings as a beloved figure:

From June 1979 to September 1979, the Armed Forces Revolutionary Council (AFRC), under the chairmanship of Flt. Lt. J. J. Rawlings...executed military officers for supposed corruption and was very popular with the radical forces.[2]

Thus, he was popular with Marxist radicals because he was "reducing prices." Nani-Kofi was eventually disgusted by Rawlings for his "neoliberalism," but he doesn't mention the brutal means by which Rawlings "reduced prices."

I become so angry when I read about these African Marxists who are so busy hating capitalism while they ignore the real human costs of socialism in Africa. I honor George deeply for standing up against them, which he did even when they were all celebrating the brutality of such "reductions in prices."

I'll return later to the insane conflation of Ubuntu, an honorable indigenous African moral tradition, with state-led socialism. But for now I'll just say that conflation was one of the worst things ever to happen to Africa, with its place in infamy adjacent to colonialism and slavery.

I also want to add that while I respect the sense of mutual obligation in Ubuntu, I also recognize as a fundamental truth that no human being wants to owe something to someone else. It took a while, but after moving to Mékhé and working for my company, Ibou was able to pay entirely for his own needs. If you asked him if he wanted to go back to the old process, he would tell you, "Dedeet!" ("No!" in Wolof.)

Every single day he lived in a world in which it was hard to have dignity. People must always, always ask for money, or be asked for money. It's constant hustling. Why do you think the sex tourism is so common in Senegal?

---

2 Nani-Kofi, "Against the Odds: Rawlings and Radical Change in Ghana," interview by ROAPE, *Review of African Political* Economy, https://roape.net/2016/12/01/odds-rawlings-radical-change-ghana/.

A French person on a government retirement income, a pension, can live like a rich person in Senegal. So you have these old men, with one foot in the grave, who keep showing up on the beaches. Because they're technically poor in France, they receive government stipends. In France, they're big-time nobodies, living in government housing projects. But those same pensions allow them to live like gods in Senegal.

In Senegal, even a French person on welfare can afford to buy (I apologize for the bluntness) "fresh meat." The retirees come down in droves for the sex tourism. So you have these young women who are barely the age of the French retiree's grand-daughters chatting up French men for just a couple dollars at the end of the day.

These perverts are living *la vida loca*, with all the respect and attention our society, too often unrightfully, grants to perceived wealth. In their own countries they would be nobodies.

But it is not just men. You also see some older ladies, some even in wheelchairs! No man in their country of origin—which might be Italy, Spain, or France—would look at them, much less acknowledge them. (I'm not saying it's right to judge anyone this way, but that's the way it is.) But they come to Senegal and... oh my god. The next thing you know they're saying, "Oh, my husband..." and pointing to this guy who is an Adonis. I mean, we're talking super-well-built men. Beautiful men.

Are you kidding me? But you know, this woman feeds his whole family—for a few dollars!

It's just so sad. The whole thing is so very sad. I believe that anyone can find love across any age range or cultural boundary (I myself am married to a man who is fifteen years older than I am and from a different culture), but that is not what is happening here.

None of these people want to live this way.

◇◇◇◇◇◇◇◇◇◇◇◇◇

MY GRANDMA

I was born in Senegal, about eighty kilometers south of Dakar on the Atlantic coast in a small town called M'Bour.

Many defined me as a *"yaroo mam"* child, a Wolof expression that means "raised by her grandma." It also carries a second meaning of being spoiled—you know, because of the way adoring grandmothers tend to dote! It was true in my case.

When I was tiny, my parents left me behind and went to Europe, with a promise to return to me. I spent the next few years with my grandmother. I felt so loved, trusted, and respected by her. She thought the world of me. She would say things like, "I can see the universe in your eyes."

She thought I was very smart. She would tell her friends, "My Magatte could sell and deliver you, and you would not even be aware of it. Her mind and wit surround her like a blanket."

I slept in her bed, just me and her. We were such close companions.

While other young girls my age were compelled to learn how to take care of the home, cleaning and cooking, I would spend my days outside leading packs of boys on adventures. Our days were filled with hunting and fishing expeditions.

My grandmother's home was a few blocks away from the ocean, so we used to go to the beach, play with the fishermen, and "catch" fish (we would beg the returning fishermen to dump their unsellable fishes into our buckets). We would cook the fish ourselves, with the spicy onion sauce courtesy of my grandma.

My friends and I brought our slingshots to the forest. We were always working out new strategies, like the best trap to get birds. We perfected a system with rice, a stick, and a big bowl. We would poke a stick into the sandy ground, perch a tilted bowl on the stick, and then attach a cord to the bottom of the stick. For bait we used some grains of rice or millet. We would gather in a nearby bush, the far end of the cord in hand. To ensure silence was maintained, we would "talk" to each other using hand signs. The birds would come in to eat the grains of rice, and the person holding the cord (usually me) would then pull the cord with a sharp and decisive movement, trapping them.

I was a master at slingshot until one day I tried to hit a bird, but the bullet-stone hit the branches of the tree. It ricocheted and hit me right in the middle of my forehead. I fell on the ground on my back, with all four limbs spread out. I was totally out of it for a while, while my friends laughed their asses off. After that incident, I decided the slingshot was not for me anymore.

Another time I was burned while building a fire to cook the fish we caught. I still have a huge burn mark on the back of my right upper thigh.

These were only two of the many accidents that happened to me. If you saw me as a child, you would think that people were beating me all day long. The truth is, there is a price that comes with having freedom. When you have freedom and do things on your own, accidents will happen. But whatever doesn't kill you makes you stronger, I guess.

That is perhaps a little too easy to say. One day I was, as usual, out and about, playing with my band of boys. We had decided to play soccer on the neighborhood's soccer field, which was just across the road from my grandma's house.

There was an electrical pole near the field that provided electricity to the stadium. For reasons I don't recall, the boys were all lined up when the pole fell, crushing maybe a half-dozen boys, maybe more. My best friend died. I can still remember that sight because his head hung loosely—it dangled from his shoulders. I didn't know exactly what that meant, but when I asked I was told that everything in him was broken.

I don't know exactly how many others died, but I recall that for hours after, we watched the horse carts go by with the bodies for the morgue. I would cling to my grandmother's skirt each time a procession walked past.

When my parents heard about it, they said, "Okay. Done. You're joining us in Germany."

Before I left, Grandma took me to the bedroom, sat on the bed, and pulled me lovingly toward her. She was comforting, but I could tell she had something very grave to tell me. All of a sudden, I felt it might have to do with this upcoming departure of mine, which people around me had been talking about.

"You will soon be leaving for another country to be with your parents," she said.

"You are coming too. Right, grandma?"

"No, *dom*," which means "No, my child" in Wolof. When she said that, my heart sank. The little girl I was became very scared and agitated. All I could think was *No, no, no!*

I must have said some terrible things about not wanting to be with my parents because I remember her disciplining me. "Do not talk about your parents in this way!"

Then I remembered my father's last visit and how he had said I was going to be with them soon. It was all starting to make sense. But I hated what it meant.

My grandmother spoke to me. "You are going to go to this new country, where most people will not look like you. Most people there will speak a language that is not like yours, and you will be going to school." My whole body was starting to tense up and get more and more rigid. It sounded very frightening.

"What do you mean, Grandma?" I asked with round eyes and a frowning forehead.

"I know it sounds scary. But when you get there, I do not want for any of those things to *intimidate* you." I could tell she chose that particular word very carefully by the way her eyes were looking deeper into my eyes, and her voice was more commanding than I had ever heard it.

My grandmother had always negotiated with me. She never imposed anything. Even when I provoked a bad situation, picking a fight with one of my friends or being naughty to another, her approach was always to support me in public but to later discuss the incident in private. She would also try to get to the bottom of what was going on, listening to my side of the story and reasoning. Sometimes she would change my mind on something; sometimes I would change hers. And sometimes we would agree to disagree. I was always free to take or reject her advice and opinion; I was very much a free-range child.

But this time, her advice was clearly nonnegotiable: "Do not let any of it intimidate you!" she repeated. "Even if most will not look like you and will have a different skin color, they are still humans, and you are a human being. The different language you will find them speaking is still a language spoken by humans, and you are a human being. You have never been to school and have no experience of it, but going to school is what little humans do, and you are a little human yourself. So anything they can do, accomplish, and be, you, too, can do as much, if not more. I am your grandmother, and you are my *nene* ("baby love"). You come from a powerful and respected family. Your ancestors are amazing, and no one is better than us.

"I will always be with you, even when you are there, as long as you keep me here and here," she said, pointing to my heart and mind.

In doing that, she entered my heart, never to leave. She has been gone for more than twenty years now, and it is as if she has never left my side. I miss seeing her, though, and feeling her warm hugs and comforting voice.

The day to leave for Germany came. I do not know how many adults were there to take me away from my grandmother. I refused to get in the car that was going to take me to the airport. Instead, I was on the ground, throwing the most horrible tantrum ever while hanging onto my grandma's "*grand boubou*" (the traditional long outfit) as strongly as I could in a desperate attempt to stay. The poor woman was almost naked as I pulled on that skirt with the last energy of the doomed.

Eventually, I was put into the car, with my eyes full of tears and my heart full of sadness and anger. I do not remember anything from that trip, despite the fact I had never been on an airplane before. All I remember was how I felt...and thinking of Grandma.

I remember, though, after arriving in Germany, I was walking down a hallway at the airport. A lady passed us by, and the person who accompanied me asked me if I knew her. I shook my head. "No. A Black *Toubab* perhaps," I said, meaning "a Black White person" in Wolof.

But after she passed us, the woman turned around and came back to us. She came up to us and asked me if I recognized her. There was nothing in my heart for her. I said, "No. I do not know you."

She said, "I am your mother."

CHAPTER THREE

Toog di jàmbat te defoo dara du maye dara.
(To sit and complain without doing anything will
not achieve anything.)

◇◇◇◇◇◇◇◇◇◇◇◇◇◇

WE DROVE HOME TOGETHER. There was snow, and it was cold!

I remember finding the apartment so small. I was not used to small spaces. Back home in Senegal, I lived on a huge family compound made of many concessions where my relatives lived. My grandma's concession was big, with a spacious court-yard in it and a big, majestic mango tree right in the middle of the courtyard. It was a favorite place to lounge and nap after lunch and dinner.

And then these two strangers appeared: two little girls, younger than me. They were really cute. They looked familiar in the sense that they, too, were little Black girls, with the same braids that I and the little girls back home had. But something in their demeanor was so different from what I was used to from my friends back home. I could not quite put my finger on it. In any case, I will never forget how excited and jealous I was at the same time when my parents told me they were my sisters, one about three years younge and the other about five years younger. I was surprised to see them—somehow I had not been aware of their existence.

I don't remember my mother visiting me back home in Senegal. I remember my father coming back to bring me a life-sized doll, but I don't remember him saying anything then. My family back home had never shown me pictures of them or told me about them. I was excited but also betrayed; it felt as if my parents were creating another family behind my back.

It took a while for everyone to adjust to our newly reunited family. My sisters remained closer to each other than they were to me. I always felt like an outsider.

School was a whole other story. I was absolutely miserable. I was surrounded by white faces. Curious pairs of eyes looked at me as if I was from another planet. There was no animosity in their attitude, just honest surprise. I did not speak German. I absolutely hated the fact I could not get up and play when I wanted to. The whole thing felt very constrained. No freedom. And I had to wear shoes. Back home, whenever I had to wear shoes I would "lose" one shoe so I wouldn't have to wear the other one. But there in the snow that strategy didn't feel so wise.

We were in a classroom of eight children with two teachers. I really liked the two lady teachers.

My grandma had been right! She had predicted most of these people would have a different skin color from mine. She had predicted they would be speaking a different language from mine. She had also predicted that these kids would go to school, something I had never done.

I thought surely if she had been so right in her predictions, then the next part of her prediction would be right as well. "Different skin color is still human skin. That different language is still a language of humans. They are humans, and so are you. And what they call school is where little humans go. And you are a little human too…do not be intimidated," she had said. "Just believe in yourself and get to work."

I took one step on my own. As I would in all the schools I would attend, I sought cues to determine who the school bully was. And I punched him in the face, just to put everyone on record about the new social order in the school.

(In my adult social and business lives, I have continued to fight bullies.)

That task out of the way, I followed my grandmother's advice, and within a few months, I had become the best in my class and was speaking with a flawless German accent. I even had a little boyfriend, Jochen, a cute little blond boy. He loved sitting next to me, and we would hold hands any time we could.

As is usually the case, though, I was learning more outside of school than in school.

My father was teaching me a simple philosophy of life. It has served me every day since. I am his firstborn and a woman, but contrary to the popular cliché, my father never made me feel that he wished his first child had been born a boy. My father always made me feel that I was his best friend and his everything. He always positioned me so high up that honestly I have always been quite afraid to fail.

A lot of who I am today also comes from that starting point. My parents were not entrepreneurs, but their thinking was entrepreneurial. My father told me never to come to him with a problem unless I also had a solution. "It doesn't have to work," my father said, "but you must think about solutions."

My parents believed that no matter what is available and where you are, you should "turn everything that surrounds you into things that work for you."

My lifetime mantra is to "criticize by creating." That encompasses this notion of entrepreneurship. We always have three choices when faced with a problem:

- **Option One:** Sit. Do nothing about it, and pretend the problem does not exist.
- **Option Two:** Sit and talk about it, but still do nothing about it.
- **Option Three:** Do something and change the status quo.

In Germany, I also formulated a question in my mind, a question I would ruminate over for decades. Learning the answer to this question became a driving force in my life.

In Africa in the 1980s, most were poor. A few people maybe had a car or a truck, but if they did, it was almost certainly rickety and unreliable. Most still used horse carts. The only person I ever heard of driving a Mercedes was the president of the country.

But in Germany, my little girl eyes were seeing that almost everyone had a nice car and a nice house. The stores were filled with piles of fine goods, and there were people busily buying them. Even the taxi drivers drove Mercedes cars!

When we would return to Senegal to visit, I always found the same place: dirt streets, horse carts, tiny stores with pitiful stocks. No progress. None.

I was only eight years old, but the question was obvious, and it pressed upon me: why are Africans so poor? Why are Germans and other Europeans so rich?

After two years in Germany, my family decided to move to France. I thought, *Are you kidding me?* Just when I was starting to get comfortable with my new life and place! *Really? What is this?*

Fortunately, the move to France was not as traumatizing as my move to Germany had been. It was still Europe, and by then I was used to different-skin-color people and going to school. Even if German was not French, I was not at much of a loss because my parents spoke French to us at home, as well as Wolof. The only difficulty was in the sense that speaking a language is hardly the same as mastering it at the academic level. More vocabulary and better grammar are needed.

In any case, it only took me two weeks to find Régis, the school bully, and punch him in the nose.

After that, and following grandma's advice, I got to work. Within a few months, I had caught up with everyone else and become the best in my class. Now I had two little boyfriends vying for my attention, Olivier and Bruno. We established turns as to who would get to hold my hand during field trips.

I was forced, of course, to follow the French way of education, which meant that by the time I was fourteen or fifteen, my future would be largely decided. Really, you don't get to make the decision; your grades make it. The good students continue on to what most people call the "general path," which is like an American high school. The less-academic students are usually pushed into technical-vocational schools, where they spend time alternating between the workplace and the classroom.

Because I was dubbed "a very good student," I took the "general path," which is also called the "royal path" because if you follow it, then you can do anything you want. The best business schools come for you—the best universities too. And the best engineering schools are looking for you.

Even in the general path there are rankings, though. The very best of the best go through the scientific path. They take the BAC Scientifique, the scientific GED. That's the one I took.

At first I chose the engineering path, but then I realized that maybe I wanted it just because it would be cool for my dad. I'd been a tomboy all my life, and I have this philosophy of being a tomboy. I don't want to be so "girly." I was like, "I'm not going to go where the girls are. I'm going to go where all the boys are."

But eventually I thought, *You know, I'm not excited about doing so much math and physics. That's really not what excites me.*

I also knew that in engineering, a lot of the students I would compete against would be kind of one-sided. I wanted to speak languages. I wanted to travel. I looked at the people I would have to spend my life with and realized, You know what? That's not really me.

Now keep in mind, this was when I was fourteen or fifteen. But I didn't have much time. By the time a student is fifteen or sixteen in France, the decision about a career path had better be made.

The most glamorous paths were engineering and business school, and I went with business school. Business school was okay for me because I loved sales. I'm a natural salesperson. But then I started looking at all the classes we were going to have to take, and it didn't feel right. It felt static. That's the way I put it. It was more managerial than entrepreneurial.

Believe it or not, at that point I didn't even know the word "entrepreneur"—but I knew I wanted to run the show. In my family, when I was asked what I wanted to do, I would always say I wanted to build a business for which I would be the CEO. My sisters would help run the company. My family was delighted with the idea. And it was the one that inspired my mind and my desires.

In business school, each student was assigned a mentor. Mine was the head of a major national bank. He and I decided I would be a trader because I loved the energy and fast pace of the trading floor. Well, it turned out his bank was a national bank but one that had branches all over the world. I was around nineteen at the time, and my mentor said he wanted me to spend all my summers in Chicago. I would get my career on track. My mother said no. She wanted me to stay closer to home.

My dreams were shattered. I was eager to move to the US each summer to try trading. I don't know how long I would have lasted, or if I would have liked it. But my mother's decision prevented me from going and living my dream at the time.

I said to myself, "From here on I'm going to do what I want to do." That was the beginning of a series of events that led to the big clash. They wanted to control my life. I was too independent for that. Moreover, I realized that as long as my mother had access to or control over me, I was neither safe nor could I ever find happiness.

Ever since I had landed in Germany and hadn't recognized my mother when I was a little girl, our relationship had not been a positive one. My father had been very fond of me, and she had been jealous of his affection for me. She almost treated me with the vindictiveness of a co-wife (first wives are rarely kind to co-wives in Senegalese polygamy). I experienced it as an extremely emotionally and physically abusive relationship, year after year. Beatings and being locked in a dark, windowless closet for entire days without food were routine. I don't recall my mother ever hugging me once in my life.

I'll give one of many heartbreaking examples: when I went for my baccalaureate, I scored 19.5 out of 20 on my Latin exam. When I asked the grader why I lost half a point, she replied, "That would have been perfection, and I don't believe in perfection." All the other graduates had families there to celebrate their achievement after their exam or comfort them if it did not go so well for them. That day, the official rule was that graduates would go in alphabetical order. With the name of "Wade," I was the last one to be examined. Of course, no one was there waiting for me when I got out of the examination. I took the bus alone back to my home after my academic victory. As is natural for any child, I was hoping to have my family celebrate my achievement with me and praise me for doing well (or at least ask me how it had gone). Instead, when I got home, she immediately began beating me on the head with a big metal ladle, screaming at me for getting home late and accusing me of being out fooling around. I probably had the best score in the district, and instead of getting any kind of recognition from my family, I got another brutal beating from my mother for no reason at all, once again being accused of something I was not guilty of doing—and once again not receiving the normal love that a parent typically provides for her child.

I won't go into more tedious detail on the years of abuse here. As far as I'm concerned, it is between her and God now. I came to the realization that if I did not escape then, I would never get out. At best I would be a dead soul having to surrender all my hopes and dreams to her tyrannical control. I also feared that I might be a dead body as a result of more physical abuse.

My father tried to mend fences between my mother and me after I left. I was working at a bank in Orleans. When I left home, the head of the bank allowed me to stay in one of the bank's apartments near the bank. After a week or so my father came and begged me to come back. I told him I could no longer tolerate my mother's treatment of me. I wanted to believe him, but I was dubious that he had the strength to fight her. My instinct was telling me there was no hope, but I agreed to come home that weekend. On Friday night I took the train to Chartre with my luggage, planning on returning home. But when the train stopped at the platform, I found that I couldn't get off the train. I was afraid of my mother's viciousness. I saw my father on the platform looking for me when the train stopped. Our eyes met briefly as he saw me waiting at the open doors—and not getting off as the train doors closed again. That was the last time I saw my father.

I made the ultimate sacrifice in terms of losing my relationship with my parents. Once you make that type of sacrifice, once you're able to look up and say, "No. This is who I am; this is what I'm going to do," you're a different person. No one is ever again going to tell you what to do again.

Many African parents are confused about the modern world. In many traditional African cultures, after a rite of passage around puberty, young Africans at thirteen or so would be recognized as adult members of society. They would have the same freedoms as other adults in their culture. There were certainly much tighter cultural constraints, but there was not the level of conflict we are seeing between African parents and some younger generations.

Frankly, I'm confused about why some African parents expect such a level of submission from their children. I know that respecting one's parents is typical of traditional parents around the world. I also know that I (and most Africans) am appalled by the level of disrespect that American teens show their parents. At the same time, I am familiar with traditional African examples in which children were respected. For instance, there is a strong tradition of Sufi leaders who were known for being very respectful of children. There are anecdotes of both Tierno Bokar and Cheikh Amadou Bamba having respectful conversations with children as their way of educating them. My own Sufi spiritual guide, Ibou, mentioned above, is very respectful of his children. By means of mutual respect, children can grow up to be confident, independent agents within African cultures. African literature is filled with strong-willed, independent people. Chinua Achebe's work, most famously Things Fall Apart, is rightly famous for showing Africans with a full sense of agency (as of course, as humans, we have!).

Yet there are many jokes among Diaspora Africans about how controlling their parents are. To some extent this may be an eternal conflict between those raised in a traditional culture and those younger generations who are growing up in a different world. At the same time, when I see how many young people in Senegal are expected to be submissive to their parents, it does not strike me as consistent with some of these other stories I have heard about older generations. In any case, I know that we won't cultivate a generation of Cheetah entrepreneurs if we raise the next generation to be submissive.

From that point forward, I would carry the lessons I'd learned from my parents with me—and their anger and rejection. And I would hold my grandmother in my heart.

But at twenty years old, I was on my own. It was exhilarating and terrifying.

CHAPTER FOUR

Pëndub tànka gën pënduw taat. (Dust on the feet
is better than dust on the behind.)

◇◇◇◇◇◇◇◇◇◇◇◇◇◇

AFTER A FEW MONTHS, I landed in Columbus,
Indiana. I had considered staying in France but decided
France was too small for my ambitions. And I wasn't
designed for the French system: if you came from such-and-
such school, you could get such-and-such job at such-and-such
company. Then, if you kissed the right behind for a sufficient
amount of time, you could climb the ladder in a very predictable
and preordained order.

Not. For. Me.

No, I had been dreaming of this other place called the United
States of America. It was said that in that place, you could become
anything your heart desired as long as you worked hard. I liked
that! It felt like fresh air to me. America felt like the only place I
could breathe.

I was ready to work hard, but I wanted to be sure that my
rewards would match my input. I did not and do not want to get
anything less (or more) than I deserve for my work.

America was home to most of the people I revered in this
world, and Silicon Valley had been on my radar for so long. What

attracted me about Silicon Valley was the freedom of mind that allowed people to go for this thing called "entrepreneurship."

I didn't even wait for my business school graduation ceremony. By then I was already in my new home in Indiana, which, as my friends had teased, had more cows and churches than people. That was fine with me. I was just happy and excited to be in America.

Today, I am very grateful I got to live there when I did. It gave me a unique chance to experience middle America. I later found myself living in San Francisco, New York, and Austin. These are not representative of the rest of the country, to say the least.

The people I had come to be in touch with in Columbus, Indiana, were amazing—starting with Carol and Eldon Wentz, whom I call my US Family Number One (I went on to have a few more such families over the years). I can honestly say that I would not be here without them.

During my last year in business school in France, we took a student exchange trip to Purdue University in Indianapolis. Carol and Eldon were my host family. We created a formidable bond, and Carol made it clear that I was welcome to join them in America after I was done with business school. Perhaps she did not know I would take her so literally. The point is, I called her a few months later to tell her, "I hope you were serious because I am coming."

She kept her promise, and her family welcomed me with wide open arms. They made me feel like one of their six children. Carol and Eldon had created a thriving automotive repair business specializing in high-end European automobiles. They offered me a job in their family business and sponsored me for my H1B visa (and paid the thousands of dollars of attorney fees). They helped me find an apartment and were my guarantors for it. On top of all that, they looked after my emotional and physical wellbeing like any parents who love their child would do.

It was in Columbus that I learned to speak American English and not the British English of my education. It was in Columbus that I learned to eat corn on the cob and had my first Halloween ride on hay bales during a fall evening. I rode in the open back of a truck, snuggled under warm blankets on a cold night, with a bunch of other families and little children joining me. Torches illuminated the path.

That is my experience of middle America.

Within nine months, I had already straightened up their accounting of many years and had improved on a few marketing plans for the business. But it soon became clear I had outgrown my responsibilities, and Carol called me in for a heart-to-heart. I knew she wanted to talk about the obvious. She said, "You have done all the work we needed from you and more. Now, Eldon and I could be selfish and try to keep you here with us. And if that is what you want, we could not be happier to keep you. But the truth is, I think you have amazing potential. And you should go for it. Explore it and make the most out of it. There is so much out there for you that our small family business cannot possibly offer you."

My eyes swelled up with tears—the tears you have when you know the separation is near. She was right. I knew it. But I was so tempted to stay. After all, I had just settled. I was tired of moving around. But I was also twenty-something, and so full of curiosity and appetite for the world.

As it happened, I had a French boyfriend who had followed me to the United States in hopes of keeping me. When I told him I was moving to the US, he had said, "But will I lose you?"

I'd replied, "Maybe so."

So he moved to Columbus shortly after I did. Eventually I agreed to become engaged to him—even though I knew he was not really a good match for me. Everyone knew it. Everyone in my life, but especially Carol, was desperate for me to move on from him. But because she knew me so well, she also knew the last thing she should say is "You cannot."

Don't tell me what to do. No one tells me what to do.

So instead she said. "Listen: as you know, Eldon and I do not condone this union. Also, there is this other man you always talk about—Emmanuel, the one who lives in California. It looks like there is something there. Don't make the mistake most people make. Go to California and find out for yourself. If you come back and decide you want to move on with this wedding, we will support you even if we do not approve of it."

Again, I knew she was right. Emmanuel and I had been friends since the first night we met in business school. My class, the newest one joining the school, was being hazed that weekend by the outgoing class. If you know anything about hazing in business school, you know that it can be horrible. There are often sex-flavored rites fueled by alcohol, all on a background of humiliation. Don't even try to escape it or you could be an outcast in your own school for the rest of your time there.

Being the rebel I was, most were surprised to see me at the hazing event. But I was curious. Things were not so bad, it turned out. Our hazing had a rather good kid atmosphere with things like a scavenger hunt.

The night of the closing party I was standing outside when I suddenly saw this handsome guy. It was raining really hard that night, and he just leaned against a pole under the porch and watched me. I saw him but feigned that I was ignoring him. Eventually he came to meet me. We started dancing and talking. Then we decided to go outside again so we could hear each other better.

On my way out with him, a girlfriend passed by me and whispered to my ears, "Be careful. This guy is the Don Juan of the school."

From then on, I tensed up. I was too proud to be another conquest on someone's board. I made sure we just talked and showed no eagerness on my part. He was used to being a winning hunter, but I would show him that not everyone is to be hunted successfully. We talked and talked. I do not remember what we talked about. All I remember is those very deep, dark eyes, full of desire, over which dangled his messy hair. Those full lips, rushing with hot blood, ready to kiss…and then the sound of these words: "You are the mother of my future children." And I didn't laugh.

But I did leave. For the few months we remained in the business school together, he would go to all the parties where he thought I would be. Of course, I was never there. I did not party much. My girlfriend would pass me his message: "Say hi to the mother of my future children."

He left for the United States a few months after we met. He was not to see me again until five years later when I came into his sight from the top of the escalator at the airport in San Francisco. I did not know if I would recognize him, despite the fact we had spent those five years involved in a full-blown epistolary relationship.

Through our letters we came to know each other very well. We became each other's confidantes. I always knew when he was interested in a new woman or was about to break up with another. He came to know the intimate details of my life, too, both good and bad. We came to know each other really, really well. We were awesome friends. But there was also something else underneath all of that. I guess that is what Carol was sensing.

Whatever it was, the minute he appeared at the top of that escalator, it was clear: this could only be love. When I returned to Columbus after that weekend, I calmly told Carol, "I left my heart in San Francisco."

I put in my notice for my job and also for my apartment. I broke off my engagement. My ex-fiancé was violent in response, throwing me up against a wall when I told him and threatening to hurt me. Carol came to get me and told him that if he didn't leave the United States, she would report him for domestic violence. He left for France soon after. The whole thing was very hard, but it was the right thing to do.

Carol was so happy for me. She said, "Magatte, you are doing what only a few people get to do in the world, which is follow their heart."

I groaned. "But I am so scared."

"I will always be right here, waiting for you, should anything happen, or if you decide to come back."

So I left.

In hindsight, I made a huge gamble. The H1B visa I was on was not transferable to another company. I would have to start over, and I did not have much time. So there I was in California, without a job and with no place to live because there was no way I would live with Emmanuel without being married. But it all worked out. I found multiple jobs that were willing to sponsor me. I took a job as a headhunter specializing in hiring CFOs for startups. Emmanuel and I eventually married. And we even bought a home with a pool. There were many ups and downs along the way. But thinking of it now, I am thankful for each of them.

Soon after we got together, Emmanuel co-founded a small manufacturing company with another French émigré in Gilroy, just a few hours south of San Francisco. While I was waiting for my H1B visa, I helped him start his company. It was my first foray into entrepreneurship—participating in growing a business from nothing. I answered the phone and made sales for the boys: "the French guys."

Then I moved into manufacturing, putting together the books and journals they were designing and selling to art supply stores and to the companies that used them as corporate gifts. They were competitors with Moleskin, which has become a well-known brand.

The early years were hard. And fun. I still laugh at the memory of how prospective customers would be so eager to take the appointment when I was doing the phone calls to present the products. I had such a thick French accent, so when Emmanuel showed up at the meeting, the buyer would say, "Hey! You are not the beautiful French woman I made the appointment with." Oops! But it would make for a great icebreaker.

For a couple of years we had no weekends; we had no evenings. We woke up at 5:00 a.m. day in and day out and were never back in the city before 10:00 p.m. But those were among the best years of my life. I was so proud to support my husband in building his company. I remember how at first he had hesitated to allow himself to be with me. I was twenty-three and he was thirty by the time we got together. He felt he had enjoyed his twenties fully and was ready to be work-focused. He thought it would be unfair for me not to experience the nonchalance of the rest of my twenties, especially in a city as beautiful, exciting, and youth-oriented as San Francisco.

I warned him, "I am not a person like that. We build together or this is it. I am not looking to be here just for the easy phases of life together. I want to be part of something. If you do not allow us to be together now and struggle together, I will surely not be there when you are ready to enjoy life. It is now or never. You choose." I even scheduled a flight back to France to show him I was serious about my ultimatum. The day of my scheduled flight back to Paris, he was waiting at the airport to ask me to be with him.

I sometimes feel that Emmanuel was more African than I am. From the moment she met me, his mother told me that from very early on, when he was a little four-year-old, Emmanuel had been making drawings of himself and a little girl—a little Black girl. No one knew where that came from. There were no Black people living in his little village in Normandy. Yet he would always draw himself with a little Black girl. Later when we got married, as he lifted my veil, he radiantly said, "I married my African queen!"

He loved me, loved my people and the continent I came from. He internalized from very early on that we are all Africans.

Yet we came from two different cultures and countries. His France is a country with a rich economy. Mine, Senegal, is a country with a poor economy. And now we were both living in the US, the richest country in the world. My entire worldview came from those three places: Dakar, Paris, San Francisco. A part of me has always been both sad and enraged at the fact that unlike most people in rich countries, the majority of people in Senegal do not get to enjoy a prosperous life, free of daily concerns like having a decent roof over their heads and enough to eat.

It was Emmanuel, whom I affectionately called "Manu," who would always encourage me to not give up on my people and my continent. Unless you are from a poor country, I think few people can understand how it feels to watch your people suffer from poverty and the disrespect and patronizing "care" that comes along with it. Back then, I did not understand everything I understand today. I was stuck in a place of tremendous pain and often resentment. At that time I believed we were stuck in poverty because of slavery and colonialism. It was only later that I would understand that while those things have their part in why we are poor, they are hardly the only issues.

As a Senegalese woman married to a French man, living in the United States, twenty-something-year-old me was often just overwhelmed by the disparity of wealth between my country and the other two. Manu and I had been able to buy a home in Los Altos, one of the richest zip codes in the United States. Socially, we were very popular. But I knew that so much of what people saw that they regarded as good in me they attributed to my Frenchness. I had European style, appreciated French cuisine, and had the manners of the French bourgeoisie. Most Americans did not really seem to respect Africanness. There is a heavy set of African American racial stereotypes, on the one hand, and then Black African stereotypes on the other (like "tribal," "barbaric," and "pathetic and starving"). Distinctive African cultures are almost entirely invisible to most Americans, Black and White alike.

The fact is that the Senegalese have tremendous style. Senegalese cuisine is delicious, and many Senegalese have tremendous nobility of bearing and refined manners. Senegalese people look regal, poor or not. But because the stereotypes of Africans are that we are barbarians, anything good about me must necessarily be French in the eyes of most Americans. Of course, they were all kind, respectful liberals. But even then the default assumption was that Africans were tribal or, sadly, came from pathetic countries. The kindest people still tended to think of me as from a culture in which our children were all starving.

Yes, Africa is the poorest continent—and yet we also have a middle class, an upper class, art, culture, technology, manufacturing, etc. We are not where we want to be by a long shot, but we are not all flies-in-our-eyes UNICEF posters.

Still, it was useful to know that most Americans held these African stereotypes thanks to generations of tribal photos from

National Geographic and countless fundraising images from UNICEF and other well-meaning charities. I needed to know what I was up against in order to fight it effectively.

But before I was ready to fight it, I first went through a phase of avoiding the issue. I convinced myself that this was not my cross to bear or injustice to fix. It was so big; it felt so unsolvable. And who was I to try to fix it? I, too, had a life to live. I deserved to live my life—to build a life.

And yet…why can people who are born in North America or Europe just go about enjoying their lives? Their only job in this world is to build a good life for themselves and their families. Why was it that I, on the other hand, could not just do that? It was not fair. It was damning and daunting.

Manu reminded me that no one gets to choose the place of their birth. In the end we are all one. He would say, "I get it. You feel unfairness. Meanwhile, I feel guilt. We both feel there is a great injustice. That means there is a wrong to right. I do not know what your part in all of this is yet, but I know there is one. Until we figure it out, you must keep your heart open. You must keep believing in yourself and your people, like your grandma said."

He knew that hearing her mentioned always brought a great dose of balm to my heart and filled me up with courage, even when I did not feel like it. So I would dust myself off and accept that there was something that needed to be done. I did not know how to respond yet, but I would keep my mind and heart open.

Then something happened. On a beautiful Saturday I decided to take a car ride down the Northern California coast, on Highway One. It was a glorious afternoon. I was alone in my car, driving along the winding road that is perched up high, with the majestic Pacific Ocean below spreading as far and wide as the eyes can see. The warm sun was hitting my face. I had Youssou N'Dour, a Senegalese Grammy Award winner, blasting in my car.

All was going well. I felt a tremendous sense of accomplishment. Emmanuel and I had made it through the early days and years of his business. We had worked really hard, and it had paid off.

After a year or so helping the boys start their business, I had moved on with my own career, working mainly as a headhunter in finance. I took a job with a multinational recruiting firm specializing in finance (then called Accountants On Call, or AOC, and now called Ajilon Finance, which is part of Adecco, a huge multibillion-dollar company). I picked it because my territory was going to be Silicon Valley. I loved the idea that I would be working with startups. Soon I came to work with customers like Google and Netflix before they became household names. At the time, these companies were in tiny little nowhere offices. No one knew what they would become. I was doing very well for myself. Very well.

To think that at first my company did not want to hire me because they said my French accent was so thick and my English so bad! (Or I should say my "American" was so bad, given my accent was British.) The people making the hiring decision could see I had great sales skills, but they feared the communications skills would not follow. I was heartbroken, but then the boss decided to take a chance on me. And guess what. I was Rookie of the Year my first year—in the whole company, out of thousands of people!

And it only got better and better from there.

This little girl from a tiny village in remote Africa was now a success in Silicon Valley, the spring from which the biggest economic revolution in modern history arose! Unlike the Industrial Revolution, which sprang from the increasing use of machinery, the Digital Revolution was fueled by ideas. Billionaires were sprouting up like wildflowers. And there in the valley, I was, as they say now, killing it!

I could not help but feel the warmth of vindication in my heart as I was driving down that beautiful coast. But then, all of a sudden, it hit. As it so often did when I began to feel pride and joy in myself and my work, my thoughts turned to Senegal and the people in Senegal. My mood then turned sad, dark, and defeated, just as it always did.

But this time there was something different about the intensity of the pain I was feeling. Whatever it was, it was such a violent hit that I jerked a bit in my driving and almost left the road. If I had not gotten a hold of myself in time, I would surely have ended up in the ocean down below. I was shaking, and I stopped at the first opportunity I found on a side road. There I wept and wept and wept. I was simply no longer able to reconcile the life of abundance I was afforded in the United States with the life of scarcity that existed back home in Senegal and in most of Africa. Yes, I had worked very hard to get to where I was, but still. The people back home were working very hard too. I was insanely overwhelmed and started feeling like I was suffocating.

I got out of the car and advanced toward the ridge. I faced the ocean. At that moment something happened. I have no explanation for it. But the fact remains. I just stood there, looking at the immensity of the ocean. I started to feel the wholeness and vastness of the ocean enter me through every single pore of my skin. As it filled me up, I started feeling super light, but super grounded at the same time. It is at that precise moment that I made a pact with God. I said, "God, I surrender. From now on, I vow to devote every single breath of mine to the betterness of my Motherland. I do not know what to do or where to start. Please show me the way. Please put me to use."

I got back in my car, turned around, and drove back home. Everything felt different. And everything would be very different from then on.

CHAPTER FIVE

Déggal ndigal i ñett, bàyyil ndigal I ñett. (Follow
the advice of three people, and ignore the
advice of three others.)

◇◇◇◇◇◇◇◇◇◇◇◇◇◇

GOD MUST HAVE HEARD ME. A few months later, Emmanuel and I went to Senegal so he could discover my *thiossane*. In Wolof *thiossane* means the origins of culture and humanity. When someone asks you where your *thiossane* is, they are asking about the history of you and yours. It goes way beyond just the place where you were born, extending into the culture of that place and all the people who came through it.

I had returned to Senegal regularly with my parents while growing up, joyfully seeing my grandmother each time until she died when I was a teen. One of the tragedies of living abroad is that I was not able to attend her funeral—she was simply gone.

After the break with my parents, I had not been back to Senegal. So much had changed in my life: first, moving to the US and launching my career, and now starting a new life in San Francisco with my beloved. It was my first time returning to my home country as an independent adult.

I was so excited to show Manu my country, to introduce my people, and to have him live among us. I wanted him to experience the legendary Senegalese *teranga*—"hospitality" in Wolof.

Teranga is what the people of Senegal are known for. And we even have a juice to exemplify it: the hibiscus drink!

Imagine my shock when we arrived to find the local people—my people!—kept offering to bring us Western-brand beverages instead of that welcome drink.

I was like, "What the hell? Can we have some *bissap*?" They would look at me incredulous, not understanding. Most folks would prefer Western brands to the indigenous products. That's how Senegalese showed their status. For the elite it meant buying imported Western brands, like Coke, Pepsi and Fanta, while the base of the pyramid was busy buying knockoffs of those from China, India, Saudi Arabia, etc. Our indigenous drinks and beverages were basically being squeezed out.

The passionate person that I am, I fell ill. Literally. I fell ill with disappointment in my people's inferiority complex, ill with anger at the reasons behind that inferiority complex, and ill with hopelessness. For three days, my body shut down. I was terribly depressed. I did not want to be part of this world anymore. *What now?* I thought. *We are now losing even the great things about our culture.*

The disappearance of this indigenous drink also meant the disappearance of the livelihood of the people who sold the raw ingredient—the hibiscus. With their main source of income gone, many of them (mostly women) were leaving the villages to pack themselves into the big cities. Far away from their family and friends, they would find themselves thrown into the heart of what poverty can look like in a city. At home, at the very minimum, you always have a place to sleep, even when you are down on your luck.

This was just deepening the vicious cycle of poverty. Why? What did we Black Africans do to the universe to be entangled in this miasma that seemed so deep it felt there was no way out?

I was so angry, with no place to direct it—except at myself, I guess. It manifested in my lying in bed for three days. Eventually Emmanuel, as wise as ever, said to me, "This anger is energy. But it is negative energy. You must find a way to turn it around, so it becomes positive energy and inspiration."

He was right! I got up. And then a teaching from my upbringing came back to me, the idea of "criticize by creating." No one should just sit there and complain aimlessly and unproductively.

I was raised with the idea that the only valid and respectable form of complaint is to offer an alternative. It does not have to be the right alternative, but the process of being involved in solutions puts a person in a very special mindset. It is in that mindset that a viable solution can arise.

The whole path forward was starting to make sense.

I had two issues to deal with: 1) my beloved indigenous beverages like bissap and ginger drinks were disappearing in favor of Western brands, 2) these women were losing their livelihoods. So I had to do something that would not just bring back those drinks, but I had to do it in a way that would put these women back to work.

My idea was simple: I was going to create a brand whose products would be these indigenous beverages (albeit modernized for the twenty-first-century palate). Embedded within its DNA would be the very best of my Senegalese culture. I would source the raw material from Senegal, specifically from these women farmers. I was going to call it *Adina*, which in Wolof means "life" in its philosophical dimension.

I would build Adina to be a beloved and respected brand in the West. When it made its way back to Africa, folks would be like, "OMG! We heard this is the stuff people in the West drink now," giving my people a new appreciation for our own products. I was going to "reverse colonize" my own people.

By the time I left Senegal for the United States, I had a company name, a product line with at least two recipes, and a plan about how I was going to do it. Emmanuel was so happy to see I had found a new sense of purpose. By that time, both Manu and I felt it was fair and right for me to try my business idea. I was the security valve when he was building his own business. It was my turn now. I quit my job, and together we freed up $50,000 for me to start my business.

I quickly started fine-tuning my ideas. I made the recipes myself at home, creating multiple variations. For both the flower and the ginger, I tried different levels of sweetener, different sweeteners, and different accompanying juices like pineapple, banana, or guava—or just straight hibiscus or ginger. Some of this stuff would come out a lovely purple, while others would look flat-out suspicious. I selected all the recipes that yielded drinks that looked and also tasted from okay to really great. Then I invited some friends to serve as my guinea pigs for a focus group. My first measure of success was that no one got sick.

Soon our entire fridge and all the space in my kitchen pantry and cabinet was taken over by all my samples of frozen concentrates and juices, freeze-dried herbs, ginger purée, hibiscus flowers, and the various types of bottles I was playing with.

I bought a few coolers and each day would visit grocery stores with samples. The results were quite encouraging, so I knew that I could keep pushing further.

In time, I narrowed down the possibilities to a few products I was pleased with. And then the fun part was over. It was time to get down to business.

I will describe here in spare detail all the difficulties I endured because my purpose isn't to teach others how to go into the drink business, but rather to explain my own path as an entrepreneur. So let me tell you what anyone who starts a business can expect: hard work, yes, but so much more. There are moments of terror and long periods of drudgery. There is strain on your health and on your family's peace. There is a lot of relationship building, from the CEOs who can make or break you to the high school boys who stock the shelves in grocery stores.

There is the terrible anxiety that rises as you watch your seed funds pouring from your bank account. There are sleepless nights wondering how long it will be before you have to call it quits.

And then there are the relatively few joys. Number one, remember this: if you want to start a business, you probably think it's all about creating a product or service and selling it. That's partially true, but this is a better and more accurate way to anticipate what lies ahead: entrepreneurs solve problems. Hundreds of problems—if you're successful, thousands of them.

That's all we do, nonstop, all day (and in bed at night when sleep is impossible).

That's the hard part. And it's also the best part.

I should also add that you will very quickly develop a deep and abiding hatred for those many people among us who believe that pointing out problems is a contribution to the effort. They take pleasure and great pride in saying, "This won't work because…" Rid yourself of them—quickly.

Some other pleasures are shared. I enlisted friends to help me determine which kind of legal entity to choose for setting up the business. Other friends helped me figure out the accounting and shared the labor on my business plan and financials.

I found a very talented food scientist, a gentleman who had developed all the recipes for Austrian chef Wolfgang Puck and other big names. We got along famously.

It wasn't easy, but eventually I found a co-packer—J-Liebs Foods, based in Forest Grove, Oregon. I called the company and explained what I was up to. The receptionist passed me on to the account manager, who was a wonderful man. He told me there were issues with working with hibiscus, but he also assured me it could be done—if his boss agreed.

"Jim is not your easiest-going man, but he is a really good man," the account manager told me. "This is a great company. They have been my family for many decades. My advice is you should talk with him and schedule a time to come up and meet with him. I have heard you. And if you talk to him the way you talked to me, we will probably get him on board." So I asked him to pass me on to Jim.

Sure enough, he was all "no" at first. I told him I wanted to come see him, to bring him some samples, and to discuss my plan in person because it was the fair thing to do before saying no to me. He knew I would be coming from California, and even then he gave me a 4:00 a.m. appointment for a few days later. Fine! Yep! I'd be there.

As it turns out, this is the hour when their day starts in that industry. It takes a few hours to set up all the machines and get all the ingredients out, weighed, and ready to go. Emmanuel, being a great support, decided to travel with me.

On the day of our meeting, we got there at 3:30 a.m. My eyes were full of sleepiness. I had not slept at all the night before because I was too anxious. So much of my venture depended on this man saying yes to me.

Looking back on it, it was very funny. In the waiting room, there were hunting magazines everywhere. There were gun magazines, too, and stuffed animals on the walls—hunting trophies.

None of this should have made me feel uncomfortable because I saw it everywhere when we visited Emmanuel's various relatives in France. They were all big-time hunters. In France, it did not feel frightening. But now, here in rural America, I was not at ease at all. Could it be that maybe the US media had imprinted the bias in my head that White people with guns living in rural America are all racist White supremacists? It is fascinating how stereotypes can work. I looked over at Emmanuel and told him in French, "Manu, I am scared. What the hell is this? Did you see all of these gun magazines, especially? What is this place? People like this don't like Black people. Maybe this was a mistake." I was starting to panic.

But Manu replied in French, "Everything is fine. Many in the Pacific Northwest hunt. Don't worry. I am here. Everyone in my family hunts. I will trade hunting stories with him. But calm down. You are too used to living in Northern California. These are real people, like in France."

A few minutes later, Jim Liebs arrived. He was dressed just like a hunter! But I took a deep breath, got up, and shook his hand in my I'll-crush-your-bones signature style, the way I learned it from my father. He was not expecting that, but I sensed it gave me points.

At first, I felt Emmanuel being a French man would not play well in our favor. But once again, those were my stereotypes at play. For some strange reason, I had always thought that progressive liberals like different cultures and really love European culture, with the French culture being perched way up there. But I thought it was the opposite for the people in rural America. I thought they viewed French men, especially, as Frogs (a negative term sometimes used for the French), and thought of them as cowards who did not stand up to the Nazi regime back in the day. They had to have the Americans come rescue their behinds. But Emmanuel was super relaxed, and he went straight into talking hunting with Jim. I watched Emmanuel as the two of them were laughing at their own stories. I had eased so many situations for Manu before. This time he was the one doing it for me. I was full of gratitude and marveled at the pair we made. The atmosphere was really relaxed, so I just built upon it.

We talked and we bonded. Actually, Jim liked me in my own weird way. And I liked him in his own weird way. He's a straight shooter. That's what I love about small-business America: people may have their imperfections, but at the end of the day, they are honest people working hard for what they have. I have so much respect for that.

Anyway, I could tell he was a truth-teller and that he worked really hard. He had told me to come in the morning at 4:00 a.m. to see how the production was handled. I showed up at 3:30 a.m. I think he liked that.

After we had talked for a while, I told him, "I'm going to be your smallest job."

He said, "Don't worry about that."

I had convinced him to take me on. It was so great. I had negotiated all of that, and now I really had a company, a viable business.

◇◇◇◇◇◇◇◇◇◇◇◇◇◇

Now that I had put the last of the puzzle piece of production into my plan, I decided I wanted a business partner. Entrepreneurship is a hard road, so it's often good to have a partner. When one is down or discouraged, the other one picks them up and vice versa. I saw how Emmanuel and his business partner, Pierre, did that for each other. My natural choice was Emmanuel, to which he simply replied, "I am happy with you as my wife, and I would like to keep it that way. So I cannot be your partner." Well, at least that was clear. And I could not disagree with his point. Nonetheless, the fact remained that I needed to find a partner. I had too much work to do to add many new bells and whistles, especially if someone had already created the basic version.

I sat at my desk and drew a chart with everything I wanted in a partner. My criteria went everywhere from her/his various skills to perceived morals. It was important for me to work with someone who understood that I was trying to serve a greater cause. My goal was not just profit maximization; I was already instinctively a "conscious capitalist," though I wouldn't hear about and become involved with that movement until later. Of course, a business needs to be super-viable financially; otherwise there is no business, and we don't get to do all the good I wanted to do. But that was not the end goal for me.

I wanted a partner who was purpose-driven, first and foremost. I did not want to have someone who would say to me, "Why should we bother creating a supply chain in Africa, with all the time and effort it will take, when we could simply buy the same raw material from a Chinese supplier much cheaper and faster?" I could not do that because doing that would mean the very African women I wanted to help would remain without access to a market. And that was precisely what I was trying to change.

I needed to find a partner who would not only understand that but who would be on board and help me find a way to build it into the economics of the business.

There were a few names on my list of potential candidates, but the one person whose name checked all the boxes in my criteria was Greg Steltenpohl, a co-founder of Odwalla, which had been sold to Coca-Cola a few years before. I decided he was the man to go after. As fate would have it, a friend of mine soon invited me to a conference because the founder of Tazo, another specialty beverages company, was speaking. He thought I could learn a thing or two listening to him.

When the panel started, he said, "Oh, Greg is speaking too."

I was very surprised, so I asked, "You know him?"

He said, "Yes. He invested in our company. I can introduce you if you want."

Whoa! At the end of the panel, many people lined up to meet with the presenters. I decided to wait on the sideline with my friend until all the people left. I did not want to be another groupie. When I finally got to Greg, I just told him briefly that I was working on a beverage company related to Africa that he might want to hear about. He gave me his card and said to contact him in two weeks. Two weeks later, I reached out to him. He invited me to meet at his house.

When I arrived, his wife was there as well, and she joined the meeting. She was French, so we bonded. Before I was done explaining my idea, he said, "How can I be a part of it?"

I had my business partner, and his wife joined too. I gave them 20 percent of the company, and we were off and running.

But I soon made some mistakes. Serious ones.

Before long, Greg came back to me. He said, "Well, Magatte, this isn't fair because I'm working so much."

And I said, "You're right. You get 40 percent." I would keep the majority.

But his wife, Dominique, had also been working a lot on it—as hard as we were. I really felt like everyone was pulling their weight equally.

Okay. I admit it. I'm too generous. After a while I told them we were going to split the company into basically three equal parts, though I would keep an extra ten percent for my role as the founder.

Do the math. Greg and Dominique each had 30 percent, and I had 40. And they were married. And we three were the only board members.

You have to understand. I was so excited. When Greg joined the company, we decided we were going to fast track. We knew we could raise all the money in the world for this idea. Greg said, "We can do in five years what it took me twenty-four years to do alone." And we did it.

Originally we just wanted $1 million from family and friends to prove the concept. Within a couple of months we had $2 million and were oversubscribed.

And then, as we were closing the financing—that was when Manu died.

As I write this, the pain rises again. It is washing over me.

It is the same pain I felt that day. Because I hadn't heard from Manu throughout the day, I grew more worried and anxious, with a terrible feeling that something had gone wrong. At home, I called his colleagues, the police, and the hospitals in case he had been in an auto accident.

No one knew where he was.

I wanted to jump in my car and search for him, but where would I go? Where to begin?

By early evening madness was descending upon me. To avoid it—to have *something* to do—I decided to go and pick up the dead leaves in the front garden.

And then a van pulled up to the house and parked in our driveway. A woman stepped out of it and proceeded toward me. She asked, "Are you Magatte Wade?"

I said yes. I saw a badge dangling on her chest. "Coroner." I understood immediately and ran away back into the house, locked the front door, and put the weight of my body on it to make sure she could not open it. Maybe if I did not hear the words, it would mean that it was not true and Manu was still here.

I can't let her in. I can't hear what she has to say. But I heard it. From the other side of the door, she kept repeating, "Ma'am, I am so, so sorry! I am so sorry."

The pain was so great at that moment I started to literally suffocate, so much so that I opened the door for some relief and fell into her arms. But I was still suffocating.

Sadness, pain, anger, fear, loss—they were all invading me.

I started hitting her. With everything I had. She just stood there and let me expel it. When I grew tired she carried me to the couch and sat there with me, holding me on her chest while I was sobbing inconsolably—just her and me, until eventually a friend arrived to take care of me. Later, when I apologized to the woman, she said she was the one who was sorry and needed to apologize for being the bearer of such tragic news. She had a very difficult job.

My Manu, she told me, had leapt from a bridge. He had suffered before from depression; indeed, we anticipated its arrival every autumn. But this year it had arrived earlier and was worse than usual. But I never expected news like this. It breaks my heart to think of the pain he must have been in. Indeed, I talked to many suicide survivors after Manu died in an attempt to try to understand. And what they all told me is that at some point, a switch went off in their minds, with this pain, an ardent pain that made them want to "jump out of their own skin" to escape it. Can you imagine such pain? My poor Manu.

She also apologized for not being able to take the pain from me. "You are too young for this," she said. She was an older lady who could have been my mom. As I write these words I feel a tremendous sense of gratitude for her humanity during those moments and wonder where she is today.

I am reliving this pain right now. I know there is nothing I can do about it. It will take its course and pass...until next time, for it is part of me and my story.

This experience forged me in so many ways. I am linked to Emmanuel in visceral and cosmic ways. Right around noon earlier that day, I had found myself folded in two with a terrible pain in my entire body. It was so violent I had had to lie on the couch, curled into a fetal position. Later I learned that it was the exact moment Emmanuel's heart had stopped and he was pronounced dead. I was a mess.

Manu died during the Christmas season. There was no room on the planes to take Manu home to France with me. It was a bureaucratic and logistical nightmare. Manu's mom and dad insisted I come home right away so they could take care of me.

Or, they said, they would come get me. But I did not want them to come get me, and I did not want to go back without Manu.

My mother-in-law finally broke the impasse by pointing out that there was nothing any of us could do for Manu anymore. I caught a flight as soon as I finished handling the arrangements with the funeral home; I gave power of attorney to Manu's best friend to handle the remaining paperwork. In France, we waited for Manu for days before he finally arrived. Everything was ready for the funeral, and we laid him to rest on December 31, 2004, in his natal village, where he lies facing a beautiful meadow.

Right after the burial, my elders summoned me back home to Senegal so they could help me grieve the indigenous way. They didn't want me to stay in the United States and deal with it through medications. The wise people of my country say, "In the West, people forgot that Death is part of Life. No one remembers that the moment one comes to this world, one is irrevocably walking toward Death. So no one thinks much of Death, and certainly most are not ready for it. Most do not know how to handle Death. And because you have been living there for so long, you, too, came to forget about it." I was home for a month, crying every day and trying my best to cope with my new circumstances. I missed my husband terribly and inconsolably.

For seven years we had been consumed with love and building our businesses. Children, we thought, were for a later time. And now, I could never be the mother of his future children. We were all heartbroken. His mom was learning English so she could learn to speak with our children. We were planning to send them to France for the summers with their grandmother and then to Senegal on trips with me. We had an entire future life planned together, and it was now completely shattered and gone.

Back in the United States everyone felt very sad and worried about me. But everyone at Adina had decided to let me take the time to go away, and I had everyone's blessing to let it all go if that was what I wanted. No one wanted to see me quit the ship, but everyone wanted nothing more than my wellbeing. If that meant I would stop, they would find a way to make it work.

The memories just kept flowing up and up. I had no desire for anything anymore. All I had was this pain in my heart. This terrible feeling of injustice. I was desperate to talk to Emmanuel about how I missed him. No living being or thing on this Earth could give me a taste for life again. I didn't touch any food for the first two weeks after Emmanuel died, and during that month in Africa I barely ate. Truth be told, I just wanted to die. I saw no point in continuing.

Eventually, I decided I was not going to carry on with Adina. I did not know what I wanted or what I was going to do, but I did not have it in me to carry on. I would tell my business partners and my investors later, but first I needed to gather my courage and strength and go tell the ladies, the growers from the co-ops we were working with to provide us with hibiscus. Back then, there were four hundred ladies in a dozen co-ops, with a president for each co-op. I had been going back to Senegal almost every month to help them build their capacity to produce the hibiscus I needed.

I went to meet with the presidents. They had heard about the tragedy and had wanted to come to see me, but I was taking no visitors.

When I told them I was going to quit, everyone was very sad. But what could they say? They could see I was totally heartbroken. Then I started walking away. The oldest one of them came after me. When she caught up with me, we slowly walked on together in silence. All of a sudden, she took my right arm. I stopped. She asked me to look at her. I could not. I felt so guilty. She asked again. I looked down into her eyes. Her face, despite the wrinkles of the long, hard years, also had the radiance of a true believer. I have always been amazed at the resilience of my people. Faith is magic. It makes people survive the hardest of ordeals.

She looked at me, and she said, "Child, I know you are in extreme pain. Besides losing a child, losing your beloved is probably the hardest thing. And you are still just a child yourself. Lord, this is hard. I know! I know that you are tired, lost, probably even angry at your circumstances. I am also sure your husband would have wanted for you to carry on because that is what those who truly love want for those who are left behind when they are gone. And that man loved you. He would have wanted for you to continue. And we all want you to continue. In fact, we need for you to continue. What are we going to do without you? If it can give you any comfort and meaning in times when you question your presence on this Earth, remember this: your being here matters. It is that simple.

"Four hundred of us rely on you. Help us. And we will help you too. Let's help each other. Please reconsider." She was quiet for a moment; then she walked away.

I just stood there on the red dirt road, just a few feet away from one of the hibiscus fields. Ordinarily, this sight pleased me immensely. Hibiscus blooms are so magnificent. We were flowering this beautiful land. This time, though, I was crying. Just crying. Not knowing what to do. But then I watched her as she was walking back toward the others. Such dignity. This woman must have known a great many tragedies herself. I know how hard it is living in the countryside. The plight of rural women in poor countries is a hard and heavy one. Most of us would not survive a fraction of what they have to endure. Yet I could not help but admire her posture as she walked away, full of dignity, wisdom, confidence, hope, and faith—faith that all would be just fine.

◇◇◇◇◇◇◇◇◇◇◇◇◇◇◇

I decided to carry on. What I was doing was too important. We were creating jobs in a system that strangles jobs. Consider what these women faced: of all the companies in Senegal, maybe 5 percent are operating legally. The rest—the 95 percent of companies that operate illegally—can only get so big before the government notices and starts creeping in, their threats focused on all the ways in which they are not legally compliant.

Many of the legally legitimate companies are French multinationals, with close ties to those in political office.

Here is where the trouble begins: Senegal has some of the most protective laws for employees of any country in the world—at least on paper. But despite those endless reams of words, in reality the employees are treated like crap. And they're treated like crap because they can be.

"Oh, you have a complaint? There's the door. There are a hundred people waiting to grab your job."

And it's true.

Some of these employees haven't been paid for four months, eight months, even a year. But they're still there, and they're still complaining. They go to their union and they complain. But no one will quit!

Quit to go where?

I've gone to places where you know which toilet is dedicated to the employees. You wouldn't want your dog to use it. And this is just one side of the mistreatment. The other is the way employees are talked to. It's just pure abuse.

If you come in from the outside world, that's what you see. And even if you're from Africa that's what you see. And your first reaction is, "The government has to crack down even more! More laws!"

For most of us who see this, we are rightfully outraged. And for most of us, it is counterintuitive to understand that the labor laws are the reason there are so few companies that are willing to be formal. That's why so few companies are willing to open up for business in Senegal, and consequently why there are not enough jobs.

As I always say, "If I can't fire you, I can't hire you." Would you still elect to marry your sweetheart under those conditions? Now you understand why inflexibility erases possibilities.

Of course, the real tragedy in all of this, and what I most of all want this book to help to change, is that most people, seeing White French multinationals controlling the good jobs, will come to the conclusion that "capitalism" is the problem.

I'm here to scream, "Noooooo!!!!!" We Africans are poor because we have not been allowed to create companies—precisely because of layer after layer of government bureaucracy that is profoundly un-African. It's because of layer after layer of government bureaucracy that only powerful multinationals can lawyer their way out of. Please, please, please, my Western socialist friends, quit supporting the regulatory regimes that are killing us!

◇◇◇◇◇◇◇◇◇◇◇◇◇

I spent the next few years, 2005 to 2008, working the hardest I had ever worked. When the first products came out, I was the one doing all the sales. I am sure those who crossed my path on those days will never forget the crazy chick in high heels hauling a big ice cooler full of our beverages up and down the steep hills of San Francisco, going basically door to door. "Boots on the ground" had become "high heels on the ground." But I was so happy to meet customers, receive feedback, and take it back to the rest of the team.

I traveled the United States; it was not uncommon for me to go to three states in three days. I sometimes landed at an empty airport at 1:00 a.m., but I was always ready to go on a ride-along with some of our salespeople and brokers a few hours later. It was hard, but I felt privileged to do something I believed in. I was still grieving, but it was good to have a purpose. It helped me hang on.

I would also often travel back and forth between San Francisco and Senegal to set up the supply chain for the hibiscus. To our early investors, this was a necessity because we all knew the strength of the brand was tied to that part of the story: It comes from Africa! We employ local women, and we provide them with access to greater economic independence!

It had to be done right, so I had to help organize the Senegalese women growers into formal groups. Before I arrived the farmers were "one here, one there." That wasn't going to work— not for the volume we needed. We also had to find a way to ensure quality control, which meant we had to streamline and standardize everything.

And we had one more task: we had to endure the long, complex, and costly process of gaining our Organic certification and our Fair Trade certification.

Of course, the ladies could grow beautiful hibiscus in their sleep, but the Organic and Fair Trade certifications each had their own specific requirements and recordkeeping procedures. That meant we needed to hire experts to accompany us and our growers in putting in place the right procedures every step of the way. I needed an entire team, but we couldn't afford to hire an entire team. Through my research I found ASNAPP—Agribusiness in Sustainable Natural African Plant Products, an organization at Rutgers University in New Jersey. As the name indicates, the folks there focus on African plants and botanicals, with an emphasis on commercialization. It was founded by Jim Simon, who was the head of the New Use Agriculture and Natural Plant Products Program at Rutgers.

Jim's team was exactly what we needed. They even had an office in Dakar, with a local team of experts. I flew to New Jersey to meet with him. He was as happy to meet me as I was to meet him. "You are just the partner we've been missing," he said.

ASNAPP had biologists and agro-engineers and other experts waiting to work, but they needed a customer for the products they were helping the locals grow across Africa. We signed a memorandum of understanding.

Most of our growers had tiny plots producing far too little for our needs. We needed land—lots of it. I went right to the top. I met with the First Lady of Senegal because I knew she was enthused about women growers finding independence through the sales of their agricultural products.

Madame Viviane Wade was the wife of Abdoulaye Wade, who was president until March 2012. I went to see her because Senegal has a lot of land, and I knew that she was already excited about bissap. I told her we could turn her interest into something big, and we could be the customer link they were all missing.

In the end, it was a beautiful partnership of the public and private sectors. It was so successful that the United Nations Development Program wrote a whole case study on us. Today I'm still amazed it all worked! Within three years we had everything done and in place, and we were certified. We were shipping container-loads of hibiscus to the United States.

Before long we put four thousand women growers to work. I was so proud of these amazing women. It wasn't easy, of course. Sometimes the growers made mistakes. One particular shipment almost ruined us. I will never forget the day Jim Lieb called us, furious. He said a rock in one of our bags of hibiscus had ruined a very expensive piece of equipment, and he was threatening to drop us. Not only was there a rock in one of the bags, but they had also found a dead bird in another. One of the filters was clogged with hair from the hair extensions of the ladies back home.

I was dizzy with anger and embarrassment, and I jumped on the first flight back to Senegal. The presidents from each co-op came to meet me, and we gathered in a circle under a tree near one of the farms. The air was tense as they knew my being there was not very reassuring. I had brought with me three samples of hibiscus flowers in Ziploc bags. I passed them around, asking them which one they liked the most. They all pointed to the same one. It had a rich red color and was super clean. All of them made fun of a different sample that was so dusty looking with some fine tangle of hair in it.

I then told them, "Well, that's yours." You could hear their teeth falling to the ground. "Yep! That one is yours."

I then proceeded to tell them what had happened, how the plant had called me and was threatening to let us go. "I thought we had all agreed on what needed to be done. I thought we had all agreed we would be honest with each other, so why did one of you think it would be okay to put a rock in a bag to jack up the weight and be paid on something that should not be paid? I thought we agreed we would never leave a bag unattended until it was closed. We are on a farm. A bird could fly down looking for food while you have your back turned for even a few seconds. Then you turn around and close your bag, not knowing it's in there. As for the hair, I thought we had also agreed to all wear hairnets. We bought you some. This is unacceptable. All of this simply reinforces the stereotypes people have of us Africans as sloppy and less than reliable. We definitely took a hit. And it is our doing."

They sat in stunned silence.

"I can't do this alone," I continued. "We each have a role to play. If one of us slacks, the whole thing goes down. I am fighting every day to make this work."

I decided they needed to hear the hard facts. "You have to understand what we are competing against," I said. "If I wanted the hibiscus you all like, which is the Chinese one, all I would need to do is call my broker. The whole thing would be delivered two weeks later. The whole thing would require only a phone call and cost me three times less."

They had round eyes. I was so disappointed and upset that tears started coming down my cheeks. Then one of them got up and said, "Child, cry no more. We got it. By God's will, you will be satisfied from here on." As I left Senegal that time, I knew we would be okay on that front. And okay we were. Their hibiscus was of such high quality that other manufacturers wanted to buy from them as well.

Anyone who wants to start a company in Africa, or in other parts of the developing world, should be aware that this story isn't unusual. Many people in Africa don't have an understanding of Western-world quality standards and what it takes to get there. This is not because Africans are idiots, but if one has not been exposed much to the standards of the outside world, then one does not develop the expertise and skill sets needed to perform to those standards. Even to this day, many don't understand that their standards are too low for many Western customers. For many people (Africans and non-Africans), it's a mystery how I am able to import our products into America, given the rigorous requirements expected by customers and retailers (especially Whole Foods).

Our women, on the other hand, soon mastered the laws of doing business with other countries. For one example, American customers expect to be able to call you. But often in many African countries, people prefer to meet face-to-face. We don't have the culture of building relationships on the phone. I admit it: because of my Senegalese cultural preference, I have become more and more miserable as the world is moving more and more away from direct communication. I always prefer to meet with people, but I am able to tolerate having to build business relationships over the phone. I had no choice but to surrender to my customers' will and preferences because the customer is always right. The surrender is "easier" because I was aware that the dominant culture around me did business this way. But when you are back home, where the dominant culture is to actually favor in-person meetings over anything else, you are comfortable in your zone and tend to have no idea how to accommodate the ways of another culture halfway across the world—and no desire to do so.

This lack of knowledge does not make it easy to do business with the rest of the world in the twenty-first century.

Nowadays, and especially in the United States, most people do not even want to talk on the phone and prefer emails or text messages. I wish we could get the rest of the world to re-embrace personal connections. My culture has never abandoned it, and I believe people are happier operating that way. But for now—and for as long as the customers prefer it this way—we as the suppliers must understand and follow the rules of engagement. The customer is king. The day we become the customers, then those who want to sell to us will know that we prefer face-to-face visits and will conduct themselves accordingly.

We at Adina needed to bridge the two cultures so we could do business with one another and ensure our products had full integrity. That started with making sure we followed up with our customers, even if it meant that it had to be done by phone or email. In the West, that is acceptable as proper and courteous.

And it isn't your customer's problem how you're going to ship samples. Just ship them. Ship them promptly, and make it traceable. Follow up to make sure they received the samples. And once you make a sale, stand by it. The greater the physical distance and the greater the cultural difference, the greater the need for superb customer service every step of the way.

For these reasons, traditional products are often first brought to US and European markets by someone from Europe or America. It is the same in South America. When you think of brands like Guayaki or Sambazon, it is American folks who started them. I know the founders of those two companies. They are basically White dudes from my neck of the woods in California who went to these places on surfing trips. These guys, when they see a native drink or other product they like, they come back and build a business around it. Meanwhile, the natives have been sitting on it forever, drinking Coke while letting these treasures die out.

Take Red Bull. An Austrian guy went to Thailand and noticed the natives were drinking this beverage that was really giving them energy. He built Red Bull around it. Today Red Bull is a multibillion-dollar brand.

I think it's great what they're doing—everyone should go for opportunities wherever they see them. If native people don't see the value in what surrounds us, it is our loss. If someone else sees the value, they can manifest it. But ideally we natives would be the ones introducing our indigenous products to the rest of the world. That's what I'm trying to accomplish.

◇◇◇◇◇◇◇◇◇◇◇◇◇◇

Despite the difficulties, and despite my mourning, Greg, Dominique, and I got the company off the ground. But it was rough going. I don't make excuses, but I was probably not myself for years. Maybe there were things I would have seen that I could have stopped, but I was so weak, and I let a lot of things happen. They weren't necessarily bad things, but they let control of the company fly away. I missed many opportunities to insist on opening up the board. At the time it was never a problem because I was looking at Greg and Dominique more as a family rather than thinking about the possibility of disagreements. If I had been in the right mindset, I could have taken care of these issues before they became issues.

I hope my own mistakes will provide some guidance to other entrepreneurs. First, get a proper advisor or a coach, someone who is not hired by the company. Second, don't have a husband and wife on the board. Duh.

We were also missing some very important skills on the board. We should have had an independent-minded person who was very strong with finances on the board. The chief financial officer (CFO) could have played that role but didn't because Greg had a habit of only hiring people who avoided challenging him—even when they knew he was wrong.

Soon I had to come to the painful realization that Greg was not capable of running the company. And the combination on the board of husband and wife was simply untenable.

I had already tried to gently move him into another position. I had even offered to give him my title as president. I didn't care. My goal was to turn over the functions of the CEO to a good manager who could actually execute on the functions of CEO. If that meant relinquishing a title to Greg so he could save face, so be it. All that mattered was to set the company up for success.

Of course, only the board can replace the CEO, and that obviously wasn't going to happen since there were only three of us on the board. So I started connecting with our investors because they would be my best and my only allies in my effort to remove Greg. I called the ones I trusted best and spoke to them. I said, "I'm worried. Would you do some homework and give me your diagnosis?"

One after another, they came back to me and said, "This is bad."

I was like, "Aie! Aie! Aie!"

Some wanted him out immediately. I wanted to take our time and do it right, hopefully in a way that would not antagonize Greg. We were working our way down that path when Greg and I found ourselves in a big argument regarding quality control. Just as they were doing the last round of inspections before the release of our latest production run, the co-packer found a crack in the lip of one bottle. I wanted to pull all the bottles from that shipment. Greg said an inspection proved the number of flawed bottles was beneath a comfortable threshold. Oddly enough, the number of flawed bottles was exactly the magic number—the number that would allow us to legally release the products.

This wasn't a small issue. We were arguing over almost $500,000 in product. In special cases of disagreement like this, a vote was needed.

I said, "I'm not taking that risk. You can do whatever you want, but I'm not voting to release the bottles without more evidence. And Greg, you of all people should know better." That hit hard, I know, because there had been a catastrophe at Odwalla. A child had been killed, and the parents were blaming a defective product they had released.

I told Greg and Dominique, "You are the majority stockholders. Hold a vote." But they wouldn't because they knew my "nay" vote would cause a lot of problems.

I became an "entrenched president" in my own company. That's what you call it when the CEO, who holds the purse strings, is fighting with the president.

It was vicious. I didn't want to get my plate dirty, so as a last-ditch effort, I hired a Buddhist litigator. I wanted calm, not anger. I had to pay for the service, just like I had to pay for every effort I made—while the company paid for Greg's defense.

Eventually, I realized my only option was a proxy fight. Only the board members could change the makeup of the board, but the investors could dissolve the board and install a new one. That was what I asked them to do.

Each investor's voting strength was tied to the size of their investment. That was when I discovered something else that made my heart sick. I found out that my friends and family who had made investments had all been clustered into an LLC that we'd established so that nonaccredited friends and family members could still invest in the business. Greg had named himself the manager so he could vote on their behalf! When we created that LLC, it had never occurred to me to ask to be the co-manager because, frankly, I did not understand any of the ramifications of such a governance structure. Now I know.

I teamed up with some of the investors I best trusted, and we began calling on the other investors. All together there were 160 investors. That's a lot of people.

I had one message: we have to go to battle. Some quietly declined. And some were in Greg's corner, often because in the "green world" of natural organic products, Greg was seen as a kind of messiah. Odwalla, which Greg had sold for $180 million, was their model company.

And some, I think, were playing the odds. Who would ever think that little Magatte, who came from Nowhere, Africa, would know what she was doing?

Before the official vote, we gathered commitments. When we hit 51 percent, we knew we were good.

◇◇◇◇◇◇◇◇◇◇◇◇◇

I was glad I had won, but it would be wrong to say I was happy about any of this. I was just doing what we needed to do to make the company work. I always told the investors the truth: that it was never my goal to make Greg look bad. And I gave him due credit, and I still do. I think we owed him a lot. I made mistakes; he made mistakes. He was definitely critical to the early success of the company. A lot of what we were able to accomplish we could not have accomplished without him.

I had some good fortune in winning this battle. One morning in the middle of the war, I found a brown envelope on my doorstep. It was delivered anonymously and was stuffed with facts about the Odwalla incident.

Part of the appeal of the Odwalla brand lay in the fact that its products were unpasteurized. But at some point a batch of apple juice became contaminated with *E. coli,* a highly toxic microorganism. Seventy people got sick, and a sixteen-month-old girl died.

Greg and his legal team had planned to fight the girl's parents into legal submission, but then a mysterious brown envelope appeared on the doorstep of the parents' home. Greg had testified in the trial that he had never negotiated with a government agency over the purchase of Odwalla products. The envelope contained documents that showed Greg had approached the US Army regarding a contract for his products. While doing its due diligence, the army had discovered traces of *E. coli* in Odwalla's products. They had decided not to do business with Odwalla.

When the family handed this evidence over to the judge, it was all over. Greg agreed to one of the biggest settlements ever in food poisoning litigation. Of course, that was just part of it. All together there were twenty lawsuits, with many of the settlements estimated to be $10 million or more.

The settlements included nondisclosure agreements. The information was available nowhere. But that was what I had found on my front stoop. For the second time in his life, a mysterious person had stopped Greg in his tracks with the timely delivery of a brown envelope full of facts.

Later some investors told me, "Magatte, we knew it was just a matter of when, not if, Greg was going to display problematic behavior leading to a clash between you two."

I was like, "Thanks a lot. You knew there was gonna be issues with Greg, and you didn't say anything?"

The whole affair was very instructive and very useful. I was beginning to understand that my ideas about these organic, back-to-the-earth folks who were big shots in my industry weren't exactly accurate. They weren't always what they sold themselves as. I mean, these paragons of virtue…don't you think that virtue should start with your morals?

I was shocked when I discovered that Greg's business decisions had previously resulted in such tragic outcomes—especially knowing that he had been willing to release the Adina bottles with the risk of cracks in the glass. How can you be an "organic" person when you're spewing poisonous behavior all around you—including the poison of lies? And for what? A few dollars? Because of your reputation? To protect one another's status? Was that why so many of the investors had fought against me, even though they knew Greg was wrong?

At that point, and in a fiduciary effort to conserve stability and unity for the sake of our stakeholders, it was decided that both Greg and I would remain with the company, but in different capacities. I told the partners, "I don't want to work with Greg anymore, and I do not want to be on the operations side anymore. Make sure I don't see his face or interact with him."

The new board did just that. Both Greg and I were pushed aside. They kept us in the organization to ease the public perception, but neither of us had any authority after that point. Greg was put into a figurehead position.

In my new role, I would take control of the Adina Foundation, a nonprofit foundation funded by the for-profit side. That included a new office where I would rarely cross paths with Greg. Meanwhile, Dominique was fired.

I was so happy to be free of the production and sales effort. I was done. Worn out. Of course, it wasn't long before new issues arose. It never is.

One of the investor groups that bought their way in was managed primarily by John Bello. His claim to fame is that he is the founder of SoBe, which had been bought by Pepsi. Through his investment firm, Bello also brought the PepsiCo people on board. (Pepsi has an investment firm as well, and they invested in Adina.) Roger Enrico, the former chairman of PepsiCo, was also on the board. And we had a representative of Peet's Coffee on the board.

We brought in these heavyweights because by this time, we were a major national company. We had raised more than $30 million in capital. The people loved us. We had coast-to-coast distribution. But then the investors got into a big fight.

What nobody anticipated was Bello and his megalomaniac, bigger-than-life personality. He had brought onto the board his compadres—his Pepsi pals. That gave him a tremendous amount of clout. But with big egos, it was all fighting, all the time.

Bello really wanted Adina to be SoBe's next brother. So get this: Bello eliminated the culturally relevant branding that I had helped to develop and replaced it with a monkey, seemingly pandering to the worst stereotypes about Africa. To me that was a huge insult. Imagine going from a brand designed to change stereotypes about Africa to a brand that reinforced some of the worst stereotypes about Africa. I was disgusted.

It looked like a wannabe SoBe. Even our new bottle. Our own custom-made bottle, with beautiful carvings and everything, was dumped. He sold all the supplies for cheap—millions of bottles—and created an entirely new bottle. The brand went from very cosmopolitan to a rough, cheesy version of SoBe. First the hibiscus beverage went away, replaced by a lightly hibiscus-flavored tea. Then they dropped that product line—and the last of the original four thousand women growers.

Everything I had fought for was gone.

Eventually I told them, "Adina is dead to me. This is not the company I founded." But, of course, I still wanted it to succeed, if for no other reason than because so many had believed in me enough to invest in it. I just carried on and tried to put the foundation into place. But even that wouldn't last long.

The company started losing customers one by one. They were targeting new types of customers because the customer base I had built—the cultural-creative demographic—didn't respond to the new branding. They didn't like the fact that the authenticity was gone. "Magatte is no longer there," they said. "So forget it. We're done. And this new branding sucks."

They were right. Adina removed from their product line all the beverages that were there before, the bissap and all that, and made it a SoBe-like drink.

Bello knew that. He wanted it that way. One day, during a board meeting, he retorted at me, "Don't fool yourself. We're just selling water and sugar."

ORIGINAL ADINA BOTTLE WITH BELLO'S MONKEY BOTTLE

CHAPTER SIX

Xel du doy. (One cannot have enough advice.)

◇◇◇◇◇◇◇◇◇◇◇◇◇

I FINALLY WALKED AWAY FROM ADINA. I was done. I wanted to start a new company with the same basic ideas— that is, to bring African wisdom and products to the world, and to bring prosperity to Africa by doing so. I wanted to do my part to raise the poor of Africa out of poverty, and that meant jobs, not gifts.

I had learned a great deal in my time at Adina, especially what *not* to do when starting a business.

I was still determined, but my experience with Adina had left me a bit gun shy with some of those well-intentioned Americans who claim they want to help Africa.

Sometimes it seemed that many believed, and still believe (consciously or not), that my people—the people of Africa—are incapable of lifting ourselves out of poverty. Others regard us as pitiful victims who require their highly conspicuous caring and generosity. Very few regard us as capable entrepreneurs who, with the right legal system, would rapidly become prosperous on our own.

Arguably the most famous American focused on African poverty during my Adina years was Jeffery Sachs, who is described in his Wikipedia profile as "one of the world's leading experts on development and the fight against poverty."

His résumé has all the ornaments that provide not just credibility but stature among those who hand out money for big "development" projects. To begin, he has three degrees from Harvard, and he became a tenured professor of economics there at the age of twenty-eight.

These days he's at Columbia University, and he also serves as special adviser to the UN Secretary General on Sustainable Development Goals. As his Wikipedia listing indicates, he has also "written several books and received many awards."

There's only one problem with Sachs, really. His approach to Africa was all wrong. It was a technocratic fantasy in which "development experts" led by him would teach us Africans how to do things right and thereby alleviate our pathetic condition.

Among his projects in the late 2000s was a series of "Millennium Villages," a dozen or so entrepreneurial African efforts run by Sachs's Earth Institute at Columbia. According to the organization's website (which remains active today, years after the experiment ended), the "project offers a bold, innovative model for helping rural African communities lift themselves out of extreme poverty." Through a "hand up" from Sachs and company and his funders (Bill Gates and George Soros, among others), Africans would "get on the ladder of development and start climbing on their own."

I first became acquainted with the inner workings of Sachs's efforts while I was building Adina. Because I was a well-known US-based African entrepreneur who had gotten African products into Whole Foods, people who worked for Sachs kept getting in touch with me.

They were impressed that I had successfully managed to create an African product that we were profitably selling in the United

States. They were trying to do the same with their villages. They kept asking, "Can you work with us?"

I finally met with one of the Sachs representatives. The meeting was as bad as I had anticipated it would be. The executive was making $300,000 a year doing his job—for a nonprofit! He told me what I already knew: that the villages were all about growing crops. There was only one problem: they hadn't considered what they would do with this harvest.

Think about that. These guys were trying to teach the local farmers about entrepreneurship, but they had failed to do any market research and hadn't given a thought to delivery systems and distributors.

As a result, the villages were producing commodities—agricultural goods like coffee and bananas and beans—which they were then dumping into local markets where they were competing with other indigent farmers who were also trying to squeeze out any tiny profit they could! In some cases, the Sachs rep told me, their products were rotting because they had no market for them.

As an entrepreneur, it struck me as bizarre that the Sachs folks assumed they would do really well at business simply because they were so smart. They certainly seemed to believe that Africans needed their technical expertise. But they didn't have even the rudiments of a business strategy for selling the African crops at premium prices. It had been obvious to me that in order to create significant revenues and profits, I would need to properly brand our traditional hibiscus beverage, then grow high-quality hibiscus to reflect the brand claims, and then get our products into Whole Foods.

Growing a commodity is the easiest part. But then you have to sell it and sell it—and sell it again!

But Sachs had no branding, marketing, distribution, or sales strategy—nothing! They were spending all this time and money on these Millennium Villages with not much to show for it. (George Soros alone gave $50 million.)

The Sachs executive didn't ask for my expertise. He didn't offer to hire me as a consultant. He just asked me to hand over everything I had—everything I had learned, and the names and contact information of everyone I had met in my years of work, my connections, my network! He also wanted me to take him to Whole Foods and tell them to buy their stuff! The Sachs team had no respect for my expertise and experience, or what it took to acquire them. They expected me to hand it all over because I'm African and I want Africa to move forward.

So I'm supposed to give it away free? They would never expect that from anyone else. I was insulted by the nerve of these people, and by their cavalier and disrespectful attitude toward me and my work.

In 2009, a friend sent me a copy of a brochure for a tour of one of Sachs's Millennium Villages in Rwanda. It was managed by one of Sachs's Columbia colleagues. Rule number one was, "Please do not give anything to the villagers—no sweets, cookies, empty water bottles or even money."

I was furious. With the help of Michael Strong (whom you will soon read more about), I wrote an article for *The Huffington Post* entitled, "Please Don't Feed the Monkeys." Not surprisingly, Huffpost changed the title, but they ran the piece as written, including my comment that the brochure "captures perfectly the revolting condescension that I feel from the Millennium Villages project."

"Celebrated professors at Columbia University," I wrote, "cannot be excused for their ignorance. When highly educated people can objectify us with a 'Don't feed the animals' sign, the only explanation is blinding arrogance. These people are so sure that they are noble for helping the 'ignorant chimps,' that they hadn't even noticed how humiliating the expression is."

For several months the article was the second-ranked Google hit on "Sachs," immediately after Goldman-Sachs. The article stimulated a debate in the African aid and economic development blogosphere, with titles such as "Should starving people be tourist attractions?"

Bill Easterly, who is perhaps the best-known Western expert on African poverty, wrote, "The real problem is that the patronizing attitudes towards the African beneficiaries of the [Millennium Villages] follow naturally from the ideas that inspire the MVs—that the poor are helpless victims and it is up to foreigners with superior expertise and funds to rescue them."

As Easterly continued, "Condescension towards Africans is both offensive AND a sign of a counterproductive approach to development." (Emphasis his.)

Nina Munk, a columnist for *Vanity Fair* and a sophisticated observer, decided to write a book about the villages. She came into the project loving the idea, but in the end *The Idealist* reads like a Greek tragedy. Sachs's ego never deflated; his big talk never stopped. But Munk saw the nonsense on the ground. She watched as the whole thing was going up in flames, but meanwhile Sachs was flying around in his private jet. He once said he could fly into a new place and learn everything he needed to know in three days. Imagine that.

Toward the end of the project, Munk revisited Dertu, one of the Millennium Villages she had been observing to gauge its success. After an expenditure of $2.5 million, this is what she found:

> For all that, Dertu still had no running water or electricity or paved roads. It had no industries or long-term jobs or anything that appeared likely to last once the Millennium project folded its tents and left town. It was startling to see how quickly Dertu's wide-open, pastoral landscape had been turned into something resembling a shantytown. Most people

lived in squalor, their *aqals* jammed together, patched with black or green polyurethane bags, and covered in cardboard, burlap bags, and plastic tarps. Slow streams of slops made their way along the narrow footpaths between the *aqals*.

The community latrines paid for by the Millennium Villages Project were clogged or overflowing, or else they had caved in; no one could agree on whose job it was to maintain them. In a ditch piled high with rotting garbage, a frenzied flock of Marabou storks ripped apart the carcass of some beast. Flimsy polyurethane bags, officially banned by the Millennium Project, clung to every brake and thornbush. The Garbage Committee had ceased to function, if it ever did function. No one knew what had happened to the 60,000 Ksh that Ahmed had given the committee to buy rakes and wheelbarrows.[3]

◇◇◇◇◇◇◇◇◇◇◇◇◇

Some years later I gave a lecture at University of California, Berkeley, to a number of young folks who were interested in solving African poverty. Some of them had just returned from a conference set up by Sachs and the UN. The bigwigs of the international poverty relief industry were all at that meeting, maybe 1,500 of them. I asked the students if they recalled who had attended the meeting. They listed an impressive bunch, from various government ministers to celebrated professors to the heads of large NGOs.

I asked if there was anyone there from the private sector. Together they recalled two names. That blew my mind. I said, "You went to a meeting where the topic is to ensure everyone has

3 Nina Munk, *The Idealist: Jeffrey Sachs and the Quest to End Poverty.* Knopf Doubleday Publishing Group, 2013.

clean drinking water and some type of healthcare and there were just two representatives from the private sector?"

Then I asked them, "Did you know that everyone—everyone!—in Africa who has money has access to clean drinking water? They drink better water than you! It is the poor women who are more likely to die giving birth, and only poor families are not able to access proper nutritious food if they choose to."

I told them poverty is the root of these issues and of a lot of the conflicts in this world. And they sort of shuffled around. "Yes," they said. "That's true."

I pressed on. "Why are people poor?"

Silence.

"They are poor because they don't have money! At least not enough money to take care of their basic needs." I paused again. "Now tell me, where does money come from?"

More silence.

"Where do you get your money from? Where do your parents get their money from?"

A few quietly volunteered an answer: "A job?"

"Yes!" I said. "You earn money with a job! And where do jobs come from?"

Nothing.

"Business!" I practically shouted. "Yes, I know some of you may believe that jobs come from the government or from nonprofits, but even in those cases the funds come from the taxes paid by companies and their employees—in other words, the for-profit sector!"

So I put it to them:

"Don't you think we should all be paying attention to ensuring that a poor country has the right environment for businesses? Isn't that a priority? But here you are telling me that you just came back from this big power meeting where these big power people are talking about how they're going to solve the problem of poverty in poor countries and there were two—just two—representatives of private business? Do you see a problem?"

The good news, such as it is, is Sachs has moved on to greener pastures, this time climate change. But in truth his reputation and his influence have both declined.

He first became famous in the post-Soviet era when he stopped inflation in a couple of countries. He was the boy genius. But then the countries crashed and burned. So he got into development economics. He wrote a book about reducing poverty and created the Millennium Villages. And they crashed and burned.

◇◇◇◇◇◇◇◇◇◇◇◇◇◇

I was getting the runaround at the Adina Foundation, which was funded by the company I had started. I wanted to fund women entrepreneurs in Africa. Specifically, I wanted to empower more people to do what I did with Adina—I wanted to give them the tools and funding to become entrepreneurs. The board was interested in funding more traditional nonprofits (what I now call "pity crap") because that was a simpler, more mainstream approach. You know what I mean—that whole "Let's help the poor natives in Africa because they can't help themselves" thing. I was sick of it.

I was embarking on a journey—one the Adina board had no interest in joining. They were interested in selling sugar water and digging some wells. I would hear about wells a lot over the following years. The next eight years of my life would be very interesting indeed.

Through the Adina Foundation, though, I met Michael Strong, who would serve first as my mentor and later in a more important role. We married in 2009.

Michael had founded a number of innovative schools and had also written a book on entrepreneurship with his friend John Mackey, the founder of Whole Foods Market. (The book also features Mohammad Yunus, Nobel Peace Prize laureate for his work on microfinance, and Hernando de Soto, author of *The Mystery of Capital*.) I met Michael through his FLOW Project, which he created with Mackey. FLOW (Freedom Lights Our World) was focused on promoting entrepreneurial solutions to world problems. Both Michael and John had originally been left-leaning, like me, but they were focused on entrepreneurship to improve the world rather than government or NGOs.

Understand: I grew up neither accepting nor rejecting the "economic development" programs in Africa. What was, was. I didn't know any different. I hadn't really thought about it.

But by this point in my life I was very interested in Michael's ideas about entrepreneurship and the importance of a good business environment, with a particular emphasis on the good that can be achieved by company-building. I certainly had enough experience on the ground as an entrepreneur in Senegal to know that the business environment in Senegal sucked. It was obvious to me that it was *much* easier to do business in the United States than in Senegal.

As soon as Michael began pointing out to me the correlation between the Doing Business rankings and prosperity, the connection was obvious. These researchers had been tracking with data the reality of my life as an African entrepreneur. If it is almost impossible to do business in a place like Africa, how are we supposed to create companies, hire employees, and grow? The connection was so obvious I was first surprised, then outraged that no one had brought this connection up before—especially not those in the West who claimed to care about African poverty.

Before learning about the Doing Business data, and information on economic freedom from Michael, I had regarded the difficulty of doing business in Senegal as just some kind of bad luck. I had taken it for granted that it was weirdly hard to get stuff done there.

We Senegalese had just gotten used to it as the way things were. It was only when I saw the pattern—nations in which it is easy to do business tend to be wealthier, while nations in which it is harder tend to be poorer—that I was able to draw the connecting lines. Senegal's poverty is directly connected to its lousy business environment.

Through our conversations and his suggested readings, I grew more and more aware of the importance of the legal system. Before meeting him I was a practicing entrepreneur, but now new ideas were forming as I connected the dots between my personal experience and the data. I spent a lot of my time as the head of the foundation with idea people rather than just doing, doing, doing.

I had met Michael because of a program he created within FLOW called Accelerating Women Entrepreneurs (AWE). The idea of micro-loans had gained favor some years before, and women around the world were having some success with it. But as Michael said when he launched AWE, "Yes, it's nice to lend a woman the money to buy some chickens so she can sell some eggs. But it's not going to make anybody flourish. Why not invest in women who are running $15 million companies? $100 million companies?"

Michael created a conference on AWE, to which he invited the world's best developing-world women entrepreneurs—which happened to include me. (The later joke is that he then picked the best one and asked her to marry him—and I did).

When we met there was an instant connection; from that point forward, we would speak at least two hours a day. That was very useful because I was, as they say, hitting bottom. I had lost my beloved three years earlier. Now I was watching my company, Adina, originally dedicated to producing authentic African beverages, as it devolved into just another sugar beverage company. But this stuff I was learning from Michael—it was energizing. I had always thought that business was business. You create a product or service, and you sell it. That was what I thought.

But now I was learning about the role of the business environment in allowing ordinary businesses to create prosperity and wellbeing. I had very much been part of the social milieu of social entrepreneurship in Silicon Valley. I regularly attended Bioneers and SoCap conferences devoted to social entrepreneurship. Investors from Social Venture Network (SVN) and Investors Circle, two organizations dedicated to investing in social entrepreneurs, had invested in Adina. I knew many of the most prominent people in this movement. But none of them talked about the need for a better business environment. Instead, we all thought and talked about how we were terrifically special, and how good we were, as shown by our "awareness." Of course, we also often talked about the evils of slavery, colonialism, and capitalism. We were a strange but not rare combination—business-oriented people who felt guilt about business and capitalism.

It was almost as if the progressive mindset prevented a basic acknowledgment of the fundamental good that business does.

I was soon eager to explain to people in my circle how important it was to work toward a better business environment in Africa. I showed them the correlation between prosperity and economic freedom. I explained how my own experience struggling to do business in Senegal was similarly a problem for hundreds of millions of people in Africa—and across the developing world.

And it all fell on deaf ears—or at least, mostly. I had a few friends in the social entrepreneurship world who understood what I was saying and fully supported my new emphasis on economic freedom. But most either ignored me or actually attacked me for supporting capitalism. The prevailing view in these circles was that "capitalism" was what had made Africa poor. For many of these people, micro-entrepreneurship was okay only because it directly involved loaning money to poor people. They were very uncomfortable with the idea of supporting larger businesses or wealth creation. Many of them hated the word "prosperity" (even though they were very prosperous themselves). I gradually came to realize that they were excited by social entrepreneurship only if it involved a rather condescending view of the charming global poor.

Meanwhile, I had always been excited by the possibility of building larger processing plants in Senegal. For me, business and entrepreneurship have always been exciting, honorable worlds. The notion that I, as an African entrepreneur, was only interesting if I was supporting poor, rural co-ops was disappointing, even patronizing. I wanted my friends to celebrate the idea of building larger buildings, larger manufacturing facilities, and gradually hiring more African managers, accountants, engineers, etc. I wanted to create a real company that was respected internationally! (Again, one of the reasons Michael won my heart was from the start he was interested in helping "developing-world women" create large, serious businesses.)

Gradually, I found myself going to the same SF Bay Area events with less and less enthusiasm. Bioneers, for instance, is largely attended by a bunch of pot-smoking hippies who claim they want to change the world but are largely anti-capitalist leftists. Although Adina had held marketing events there for years (they were our perceived demographic), as I attended their events I realized that they had no interest at all in working with me to create serious businesses in a world-class business environment in Africa. We were, to use an expression from my Sachs article, merely their anthropological wet dream.

It is very hard for me to write these words because to this day I very much like the founders and attendees of Bioneers and the warm atmosphere of the gathering. I believe their intentions to be good and well meaning. But it is through witnessing the harmful consequences of the philosophies they promote in the name of wanting to do good that I truly came to feel in my bones the meaning of the expression "The road to hell is paved with good intentions."

I just can't afford for my people to remain in hell. Calling this out so we can do a course correction may mean bruising the hearts of those who will then complain, "But we just wanted to help." But that's a price I'm willing to pay. At this point I have no patience whatsoever with people who claim they want to help Africans or Black people but who are "anti-capitalists."

If I'm trying to help but I learn the ways in which I am engaging is not helping, I usually proceed to make changes. Is the goal to really achieve actual change, or is the goal for you to feel that you are the savior of the day? These are two very different goals, which can lead to two radically different outcomes.

Which are you pursuing? There is no right or wrong answer to this question, for it is a very personal question. But one should be honest. I always prefer an honest opportunist to someone who pretends to be an ally but whose beliefs are undermining me every step of the way.

Gradually my social circle started falling apart. In some cases, my friends started pushing me away.

Prior to our relationship, Michael had written an article arguing that Walmart had become the leading anti-poverty organization in the world. He pointed to the lift it gave to tens of millions of desperately poor Chinese beginning in the 1990s as it imported low-cost Chinese products to the United States. It turned out that the much-maligned "sweatshops" were actually the first critical step on the path to mass prosperity. Even *The New York Times* came to recognize that.

Bloomberg followed up by interviewing Michael about the article and his views. He was wearing a blue shirt for the interview.

After I started dating him, I mentioned him to a friend. She must have googled him because she soon called me and said, "You can't date Blue Shirt!"

"What are you talking about?" I asked, confused.

She said, "That man! Blue Shirt!"

"Who?"

"Michael Strong!"

"But why not?" I waited expectantly.

"He likes Walmart!"

I laughed. But you know, that was my crowd. We didn't shop at Walmart. We wouldn't be caught dead in Walmart! If you had asked me at that time, I would have told you that Walmart didn't pay people enough. Walmart sold crap. And Walmart didn't respect the environment.

The fact that Walmart allowed poor people to buy consumer goods they otherwise could not afford had never occurred to me. I had never thought about it that way. I had never even imagined that low-cost manufacturing in China was bringing hundreds of millions of working-class Chinese to a standard of living that Africans could only dream about.

Back in my Adina days, my friends and I had made fun of the Walmart shoppers. We passed those emails back and forth, the ones with the pictures of the big dumb Walmart customers. It still saddens me that I could have been so ignorant. For us, it was backward people shopping at a backward place, doing backward things to the environment and people. They didn't even know what was good for them!

Wow.

I expect that many of my progressive friends believe that I fell under the spell of Michael. I'm sure some of my critics will make that claim as soon as they read this. After all, who would turn away from the enlightened society of San Francisco to listen to Mr. Blue Shirt?

But none of them have actually tried to build a real business from the ground up in Senegal. After building the hibiscus supply chain for Adina, I was certain of one thing: it is hard to do business in Senegal. I also knew my fellow African entrepreneurs, from countries around the continent, had endured the same difficulties.

It gets confusing—the varying causes of the challenge of building a business on the ground in Africa tend to get mixed together in your mind. Of course the infrastructure is a mess— highways are congested, diesel fumes stink, and it's hard to get electricity. And you have to pay a government official a bit extra here and there to get things done, particularly when wading through the absurd reams of regulations. In the end, the challenge of making your way across town three times and waiting in line forever in hopes of getting electricity doesn't differentiate itself from traipsing across town five times to get the business license.

But when Michael pointed out that it takes a few minutes online to set up an LLC in the United States—something that takes six months and thousands of dollars in Senegal—I got it.

As someone who waited in those lines and argued with those bureaucrats (and spent endless amounts of money doing it), I totally got it.

Before I met Michael and his crew, I already knew that when it comes to helping raise people out of poverty, business is better than aid, but I had to learn that business doesn't exist in a vacuum. If there are absurd regulatory obstacles interfering with business, it becomes overly onerous for entrepreneurs to create jobs and prosperity.

◇◇◇◇◇◇◇◇◇◇◇◇◇◇

Michael had an interesting educational background, including a serious background in economics. He had attended Harvard for one year but left because he was bored by being lectured at. He finished at St. John's College in Santa Fe, where he studied a Great Books curriculum. Then he went to graduate school at the University of Chicago, where he planned to prove the famous Chicago economists were wrong. Everyone knew that free markets were bad—he just had to show them. The Chicago economists claimed to be scientific. He thought that by studying their work up close he could discover the flaws in their thinking that led them to support free markets.

Gradually he came to realize he had not understood economics. That was the late 1980s, when most intellectuals still supported socialism. When he was at Harvard in the early 1980s, the intellectual debate was between Marxist advocates of violent revolution on the one hand and democratic socialists who advocated for more of a Scandinavian model on the other. Free-market economics was considered beyond-the-pale right-wing thought, unsuitable for serious, thoughtful intellectuals.

But by the late 1980s, the economic success of the Asian Tigers—Hong Kong, Singapore, South Korea, and Taiwan—was unmistakable. In the broad debate between socialist economies and capitalist economies, capitalism was winning. And then communism collapsed.

In the 1990s, China and India began taking off through capitalist projects. China, in particular, was climbing rapidly because of its Special Economic Zones (SEZs) modeled explicitly on Hong Kong and Singapore, the most free-market jurisdictions in the world. As Ning Wang and Nobel laureate Ronald Coase noted in *How China Became Capitalist* (2012), these islands of radical capitalism within China were driving Chinese prosperity.

Despite the anti-globalization movement of the 1990s, the unmistakable fact was that capitalism was clearly making poor countries rich. By the time Michael began FLOW with Mackey in 2003, he was very familiar with New Institutional Economics and the role that legal and cultural institutions play in providing the business environment needed for prosperity. Thus, by the time he met me, he had spent twenty years studying the prerequisites needed for prosperity (including his Chicago dissertation, which was mostly written under the guidance of Chicago economist and Nobel laureate Gary Becker).

Between my on-the-ground entrepreneurial experience in both Senegal and the United States (I could compare the realities directly as very few could) and his academic knowledge, we could present together a thorough account of how poor legal institutions, including excessive regulatory obstacles, lead to a dearth of legal businesses. From there it was pretty obvious why most employment in Africa is in the informal sector and why there was massive unemployment, massive poverty, and massive efforts to escape to Europe in the hopes of getting a better job.

While we can quibble about the details (to what extent is it the labor laws? The credit regulations? The tariffs? The Byzantine tax code? The obstacles to starting a business in the first place? And so forth), in broad outline, no honorable person who has looked into this can ignore the need for a better business environment in Africa—one that provides fewer government obstacles to business activity.

As I began talking about these ideas to friends, colleagues, and acquaintances in the Bay Area, I'd hear one of two responses. Some people were honestly curious and were often surprised they hadn't heard this information before. They were interested in knowing more and continued to support me. The other response was one of rejection, either ignoring or dismissing my new perspective. I was perceived as too pro-capitalist, too "libertarian," or too "right wing." I'd put 5 percent of people in the first category and 95 percent in the second.

Those in the latter category didn't provide an argument against my new perspective. Not one of them even tried to argue that the insane obstacles to business in Africa were a good thing. If they responded at all, they'd talk about the bad things that Bush Jr., had done, or the World Bank had done, or this or that company had done. I didn't disagree with them about any of this. I still agreed with them on the bad things that Bush, the World Bank, and many corporations had done. But the fact that X had done a bad thing did not improve the business environment one bit. It did not help me or other entrepreneurs create jobs. These criticisms of other issues did not stop one of my people from dying at sea. Not one.

Gradually, I came to the conclusion that many of my anti-capitalist friends were motivated more by their hatred of capitalism (as manifested by their focus on bad things X, Y, or Z allegedly caused by capitalism) than by a positive love and care for Africans.

Once I realized their hatred of capitalism was more important to them than the lives of actual Africans, I could no longer regard them as morally serious human beings. And then I had to slowly peel away from them. As I did, I saw they weren't trying to understand me and my changing opinions; it was just rejection—ostracizing.

It is important to be clear just how powerful this transformation of my outlook was for me. The burden of being a Black African is immense. Everyone regards us as poor and pathetic. The stereotypes associated with us are entirely negative. Some on the right remain explicitly racist and regard us as low-IQ barbarians. Some on the left regard us as sad victims of slavery and colonialism, exploited to this day by greedy capitalists. They want to give and give and give, but they don't take us seriously as peers.

Kenyan author Binyavanga Wainaina captured the predominant attitude brilliantly in his satirical essay, "How to Write about Africa":

> Never have a picture of a well-adjusted African on the cover of your book, or in it, unless that African has won the Nobel Prize. An AK-47, prominent ribs, naked breasts: use these. If you must include an African, make sure you get one in Masai or Zulu or Dogon dress…
>
> Make sure you show how Africans have music and rhythm deep in their souls, and eat things no other humans eat. Do not mention rice and beef and wheat; monkey-brain is an African's cuisine of choice, along with goat, snake, worms and grubs and all manner of game meat. Make sure you show that you are able to eat such food without flinching, and describe how you learn to enjoy it—because you care.
>
> Taboo subjects: ordinary domestic scenes, love between Africans (unless a death is involved), references to African writers or intellectuals, mention of school-going children who are not suffering from yaws or Ebola fever or female genital mutilation.
>
> Throughout the book, adopt a sotto voice, in conspiracy with the reader, and a sad I-expected-so-much tone. Establish

early on that your liberalism is impeccable, and mention near the beginning how much you love Africa, how you fell in love with the place and can't live without her. Africa is to be pitied, worshipped or dominated. Whichever angle you take, be sure to leave the strong impression that without your intervention and your important book, Africa is doomed.

Read the whole thing. It is the single best expression of our exasperation with how the world sees us. As long as we are merely victims of slavery and colonialism, to be pitied, where do we go? Most Africans are cynical about foreign aid. There is a popular card game making fun of NGOs and foreign aid. In Kenya there is a sitcom about the aid industry!

Poverty, Inc., a film in which I appear, documents just how counterproductive the incentives associated with foreign aid and NGOs are. (It's available on video streaming platforms.) The entire system is a joke—but sadly, a better future for us is not part of the punch line.

The business environment is terrible, and the film provides that reality-based explanation for why Africa is so poor. But for us optimists it is also a source of hope. After all, we now recognize the problem, which means we can implement a solution.

It's difficult to describe just how important this was to me. After years and years of searching and hearing all kinds of explanations, I finally had something that made sense. It was an answer that carried in its belly a promise that we—my people—could be recognized as full-on human beings.

I had seen so many Africans who became prosperous as soon as they moved to a rich country. I was one of them. Why, then, were Africans so stuck in poverty in Africa?

Because it was, and is, impossible to do business in our countries.

The day it all became clear to me and I connected the dots, I fell on my knees, crying warm and big tears of relief. It was the type of relief one can feel after one has spent the last three decades of one's life going from doctor to doctor, expert to expert, shaman to shaman, in the hopes of discovering the reason for one's illness. But everywhere you go, you are given explanations that don't add up and remedies that don't work. Just as you start to believe that maybe things will never change and that you will have to live with your illness and pain forever, just as you start to surrender to your chronic misery, your answer comes. All of a sudden everything makes sense. Everything. It is such a sacred moment of Truth revealed.

"It is not permanent, and we know how to fix this. It happened to others before, and we fixed it. Dry your tears, and let's do this," Truth said.

I fell on my knees because finally I had found the correct diagnosis to Africa's misfortune. I had found a path to a glorious African future. It was my own *Nafi* moment.

GDP Per Capita

CONTSTANT 2010 US$ Data from World Bank ©2014 Google

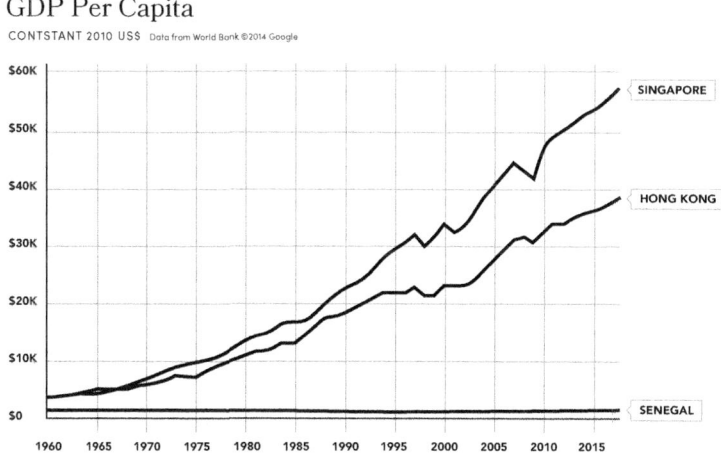

Once we diagnose the problem correctly, we can begin working to fix it. I was exhilarated by a vision of a proud, prosperous Africa. As I learned just how rapidly Hong Kong and Singapore had moved from poor backwaters to world-class powerhouses in commerce, finance, and tech, I was excited to get more people on board to bring Africa into the twenty-first century as fast as possible. In 1960, Singapore was a bit more than twice as prosperous as Senegal (US$1,400 vs. US$3,500 annual GDP per capita). Now they are almost forty times as prosperous as we are (US$1,500 vs. US$58,000). Imagine if we had the commitment to capitalism provided by Lee Kuan Yew instead of the socialism provided by Leopold Senghor!

For a people universally regarded as worthy of pity at best, who would not support Africans as co-creators of global prosperity and innovation?

As I soon learned, 95 percent of my former network didn't care. It was more important to them to be identified as enlightened (albeit wealthy) critics of capitalism. That was depressing. I finally had a plan of action that made sense, that provided hope, and I could only find a handful of people who were on-board with it?

The deafness of most people with respect to this issue continues to trouble me and breaks my heart to this day. Not one single person can deny that if African nations provided business environments that were as effective and streamlined as those of New Zealand, Singapore, Hong Kong, or Denmark (the top four on the World Bank Doing Business rankings), then Africa would become more prosperous. But in order to do this, they would have to acknowledge in a forthright way that capitalism is a *sine qua non* for prosperity and wellbeing. And that is a bridge too far.

My whole world changed. Everything I knew. The type of conferences I would go to—everything. For some of my friends it became clear that they couldn't be seen around me anymore.

What I've come to understand in the world is this: there are many reasons to admire someone, but money, schooling, position, attractiveness, and fame are none of them. For me, I care about the combination of a big mind with a big heart. In Michael, I had found someone who had both—and who was willing to join me, and who also believed in a prosperous African future led by African innovative creators, similar if not superior to those I saw in Silicon Valley.

About six months before I met Michael I was in Senegal and met Ibou, who would become my spiritual guide (as well as my factory manager, as you read earlier). I was at a social gathering in Senegal when he approached me. He immediately saw, in his words, that I "was like a candle in the wind." This was just after the Adina debacle, when the new board had replaced Greg and me. I had been involved in a bitter fight and was exhausted by it. Since my return to Adina after Manu's death, I had been building, building, building—flying around the United States to sell, flying to Senegal to organize the hibiscus production, and so forth— until the dispute with Greg and Dominique. Now it was all over. I was suddenly free from day-to-day responsibilities with Adina. I was a young widow. I was relaunching my life and recentering my priorities. Who was I?

Ibou quickly became my counselor, spiritual guide, and best friend. He had been raised in the Sufi mystical traditions of Senegal. He had spent years in meditation, prayer, and staying out on the beach having visions. But he was not a cold, ascetic person—on the contrary, he was very warm and human, with a laugh that instantly put me at ease. I can be extremely intense— but Ibou was never bothered by that. He could handle my passion, no matter how angry I was, with a gentle laugh. I immediately perceived he was a wise man. He always considered various sides of every problem, and he always took the high road of good-ness. He always encouraged me to do the right thing and to think about the long view, no matter what.

Soon after meeting Michael, I began to tell Ibou about our relationship. In some respects, Michael and I are extremely different: he is a patient, quiet, thoughtful intellectual. I'm a passionate, feisty, talkative entrepreneur. He is primarily focused on books and ideas; I love beautiful things, beautiful homes, beautiful places, and lively events. He is tall, thin, and very white; I'm curvaceous and very black. He is also fifteen years older than I am. Shouldn't I find someone more like me, at least in some respects?

In a funny way, Ibou and Michael are very similar, although Ibou was a traditional Sufi mystic and Michael is a rational Western intellectual. They literally did not speak the same language—Ibou spoke Wolof and French, but no English, whereas Michael doesn't even understand French (although he can read it a bit). But despite these differences, the two of them exemplified a remarkable sort of universal wisdom. On countless business and personal decisions over the years, I would ask them almost identical questions, and they would give me almost identical answers. They are a beautiful example of our shared common humanity.

Ibou's mysticism included an ability to see a person's aura. When he met Michael, he said that he had one of the purest auras of anyone he had ever seen. When I began to consider becoming serious about Michael, Ibou was perfectly clear: "This is a good man," he said, "and he loves you and cares about the things you care about. He will be good for you." Ibou's testimony removed any doubts I may have had about committing to Michael.

It's funny that as an entrepreneur, I constantly sought Ibou's advice. He didn't have much money, but he always had enough. He believed a lot of traditional beliefs, but he was also a very modern person.

And he supported me. He said, "Magatte, when you come to Senegal, I see you live as modestly as we do. Nothing makes you happier than getting your feet dusty in your little village."

He was right. What I eat in Senegal probably costs less than $2 a day. Not because I can't afford better. Ibou said I am content to eat simply because I have devoted my life to doing something bigger in the world.

"And I see you," he said. "I see how you conduct yourself. You have devoted your life to the cause of this continent, and it shows in everything you do." Ibou said if I were a more religious person, I would be a *Waliyy*, which in our religion means "a friend of God." They are very sacred people, very pure. I am honored he thought of me this way and can only dream to be even a fraction of that.

Ibou devoted himself to accompanying me on this journey of working on behalf of our beloved continent. Before meeting me he was a landscaper and then a night guard. He went to high school but not to college. He also served in the military and traveled to Saudi Arabia, Libya, and Benin. He was truly enlightened. He couldn't care less about the material things of this world—to a fault, almost. In addition to his wisdom, he was a paradigm of integrity, very smart, hard working, and dedicated.

It was for all these reasons and more that I made him the manager of the factory in Mékhé. Without him, we couldn't have done what we did and what we do. He expected our employees to perform to world-class standards. But he also knew how to lead them to this goal. For Ibou, poverty justified nothing. You're either a person of dignity and honor or you're not. That's why he was a leader.

Ibou was the key person in my business because he prevented me from making the mistakes common to those who are not local. He understood the local culture of Mékhé more deeply than I do, and as a religious and spiritual man, he was widely respected.

When people ask me how to do business in Africa, my first response is always, "Be humble." I'm African, but I'm part of the African Diaspora, so I must be humble because I have been away for many years and have been influenced by living in the West. I have learned things in the West that put me at a distance from those I grew up among. Or maybe it's not so much "learned"—that suggests formal education. I think it's perhaps better to say I picked up certain ideas and attitudes from the cultures in which I've lived. In order for the African Diaspora to be most effective in Africa, we need to work closely with those who have not left home to integrate the best of both worlds.

Sometimes those differences can cause friction. For example, after one particularly hard rain, only one worker showed up to the factory. I was so angry. I was like, "What the heck is going on? The White people are so right about us! We don't show up on time!"

Ibou calmed me down. He said, "Magatte, do you know why no one is here?"

I said no.

He pulled me outside to the porch. "Do you see these lines that go from here to here? You have talked about how bad these unpaved streets are. But you don't know that when it rains hard, the power lines can come down, and people get killed. It's not safe for people to be out."

It suddenly made sense. They don't have cars—they're walking from point A to point B at the risk of this! I should have known better! I'd seen what could happen with power lines!

But I was still angry. I said, "Why don't they just call us to let us know they need to wait until it becomes safer to venture out?"

Ibou said, "You're right. On that I agree with you. And I'm going to train them on that."

We are from closely related tribes—Ibou was a *Serere,* and I am a *Lebou.* He was living in Dakar when I met him. Later, Michael and I rented a home on the beach in Yoff near the Layenne mausoleum near Ibou's home. We became very close to Ibou and his family.

CHAPTER SEVEN

Mer, noonub boroom la. (Anger is the
enemy of its owner.)

◇◇◇◇◇◇◇◇◇◇◇◇◇◇

MADE UP MY MIND. I would start a new for-profit company. I would go back to Africa and essentially follow the same plan I had used for Adina, but this time with high-end cosmetics. With Adina, I had brought traditional Senegalese bissap to the West with modified recipes for American consumers. With my new company, Tiossan, I would bring traditional Senegalese skin care recipes from the traditional healers and modify them for American consumers. (The original recipes produced a thick gray mud that American consumers would never use, but I knew that the underlying ingredients—shea butter, baobab oil, etc.—were, in fact, terrific for one's skin.)

The goal was eventually to produce the products in Africa, but we knew it would be better to get the kinks worked out before moving production there. There would be no pity branding. No, "Please buy my products because you feel sorry for Africa," but rather, "Buy our product because it is the best in the world for your particular skin problem. And it is from Africa."

When I started thinking about Tiossan, I did a survey of African brands. Of the top one thousand brands in the world, only one was a company based in Africa, and that was South African Airlines, which was started by White South Africans under apartheid. The brands I did find were either tribal brands or safari brands or pity brands. You know the kind—tribal peoples with face paint and exotic masks, zebras and giraffes, or "Buy this stuff to help the 'pathetic' Africans."

I'm not denying that pity sells. You can really push people's buttons because most people do want to help. I can see why some people take this easy route. But I can also see how taking the easy route has formed stereotypes of Africans. For instance, up until the last decade, one of the most common images of Africans in the West was starving kids with bloated bellies and flies in their eyes. Again, I understand why the NGOs used such images to raise money. But as a cosmopolitan African concerned with the image of Black Africans in the West, imagine what it felt like when every Westerner's first thought of an "African" is a starving kid with vultures waiting. Is that promoting African dignity?

As I was thinking about the new Tiossan brand, I was deliberately working to create a new Afropolitan identity. In 2008 and 2009, I regularly googled "contemporary African" on Google image search. There were a few cool images, mostly from Indaba, the South African design festival. But very few. By contrast, if I googled "contemporary Asian," there were thousands of images of contemporary Asian cuisine, architecture, fashion, etc. Asian style and design had developed a fantastic area of new and exciting cultural syntheses. Why were we Africans still stuck with tribal, safari, and pity brands when many Asian cultures were represented by dynamic, cutting-edge cultural objects and trends?

Do you know why most young people around the world love the United States? It's because we have all the cool brands that inspire their day-to-day lives. It's Coca-Cola, Pepsi, Apple, McDonald's, Disney, the National Basketball Association, and all the other world-spanning brands.

I not only had to decide on my own what contemporary Africa is, but I had to create it. My ambition was to establish an answer to the question, "What does a high-end contemporary African look like?"

I created Tiossan with exactly that attitude in mind. "Just watch what we can do. We'll go head to head and beat the finest brands in the world."

I thought, and continue to think, the promise of Tiossan is great. The direction I was going in was great. Relying on the know-how and the traditional knowledge of the Sufi healers of my native country was sound.

But I didn't know my market. With Adina I targeted the "cultural creatives." It's a well-known marketing demographic brought to mainstream attention by Paul Ray and Sherry Anderson in their 2000 book, *The Cultural Creatives: How 50 Million People Are Changing the World*. A few of the characteristics of cultural creatives that the authors identified include:

- A love of nature and deep care about its preservation and its natural balance
- A strong awareness of planet-wide issues like climate change and poverty and a desire to see more action on them
- A commitment to activity and activism, including voluntarism
- A willingness to pay higher taxes or spend more money for goods if that money goes to improve the environment
- A personal emphasis on the importance of developing and maintaining relationships
- A personal commitment to helping others and developing their unique gifts
- An intense interest in spiritual and psychological development (personal growth)

In short: Whole Foods shoppers.

When I created Tiossan, my idea was to change the perception of Africa by means of creating a high-end African skin care product line. Because that was my goal, I explicitly decided that I did *not* want my products carried in Whole Foods because I knew that the body care products used by the granola-crunching hippie stereotypes of the time did not convey the sophistication and luxury that I was aiming for. Instead, my target retailers were those like Nordstrom because of their higher-end and no-nonsense positioning. As it turned out, I was able to get my products into Nordstrom.

But I soon discovered that my new positioning was challenging both for investors and for consumers. The level of unconscious, well-meaning attachment to the pity branding for Africa was quite profound.

I spoke to one potential investor, a retired-at-forty-something who was devoting his life to helping the poor. I went to see him at his penthouse in San Francisco to ask if he would join us as CFO.

He simply had no interest in us because he didn't see how Tiossan was helping Africa. He asked the questions I knew were coming.

"Yes," he said, "but what are you going to do *for* Africa? What about the wells?"

Aren't we going to dig some wells?

Can't we build some schools?

How are you actually going to help Africa?

These were typical questions. When I heard them I would think, *What are you smoking? We're creating jobs in Africa and high-end products that will cause people to see Africa in a whole new light. What we are doing can result in long-term improvements for the lives of people back home!*

My goodness. How did we get here? How did we get to believe that the only way to help Africa is by digging wells and then building some mud schools? Creating jobs had never entered this gentleman's mind.

This man had made a lot of money. He was a former Silicon Valley CFO who was now devoting his life to building schools in poor countries. Because that's the only way to help poor people, right?

But what about jobs that would allow people to provide for their children's education? And what about the dignity that comes from that? That conversation was so telling to me. I walked out thinking, *Oh my god.*

But here's the real crux of the issue: people like him are the ones who declare they care about Africa. But when I went down my new path, they were nowhere to be seen because they simply could not relate. I sometimes say they have no receptors. They can hear you, but it's like talking to a marshmallow or punching a cloud. They were like, *Huh?* They couldn't understand.

So the cultural creatives were not excited by Tiossan and its assertive message of African excellence.

On the other hand, mainstream business types often had highly negative perceptions of Africa; they understood my purpose, but it was basically impossible to convince them we could create products in Africa that could compete with the premium products in the world. At least theirs were business decisions. Frustrating, sure, but understandable.

I like to think maybe it was just an idea ahead of its time, though we did okay. Our lotions, washes, scrubs—they were all doing pretty well, but sales were not as strong as I'd hoped.

Some years down the road, I was able to connect with Arianna Huffington's organization. I had created a line of sleep-enhancing products for Tiossan. At the same time Arianna had published a book on the "Sleep Revolution," a new marketing idea promoting the mental and physical benefits of proper sleep. Tiossan was the perfect partner because we were a purpose-driven company in the beauty industry—and we had sleep products. We sold candles, bath salts, and other products, all designed to help you sleep.

Her people told me, "We love that your products are so well aligned with her book's message." We agreed to partner, so I changed everything around and created "Sleep Revolution, brought to you by Tiossan."

Months later, when we were finally finished with the product reset, no one at Arianna's office would pick up the phone or answer emails. No one. Eventually I read in the news that Arianna, who had four years before sold HuffPost to AOL, was now off and running with something called Thrive Global, a new company that focuses on reducing office burnout.

So there I was with all these products I couldn't do anything with because they were co-branded.

That was very, very hard.

And to be honest, by that point I was tired, I was burned out. I had been working on Tiossan for eight years. What else could I say? My "friends" had rejected me. Tiossan wasn't a good fit for the cultural creative demographic at Whole Foods, but it was also not a good fit for the upscale clientele of Nordstrom. Back then they had a hard time relating to natural products. Whole Foods customers didn't relate to "Africa chic," and the Nordstrom folks didn't get the "Africa-conscious" angle.

Some good things had happened, though, and we'd had some good moments, but my soul wasn't happy. I was beaten up, and I realized I needed to put Tiossan to sleep for a while. I was more comfortable with my decision, I think, because I always knew it would never go away altogether.

I also believe that what was supposed to happen, happened.

CHAPTER EIGHT

Kilifa day folliy noppam fal ay gëtam.
(Elect the eyes and dethrone the ears.)

◇◇◇◇◇◇◇◇◇◇◇◇◇◇

W HEN I SHUT DOWN TIOSSAN, I felt awful. I was exhausted and depleted. I was no longer the wunderkind of African entrepreneurship. But Michael and I were now living in Austin, Texas. It was the perfect moment for starting over. I would take my learned lessons and begin again because that's what entrepreneurs do.

Part of what I was formulating anew was my vision as a co-creator of prosperity and innovation for Africa. Through Michael, I had attended many libertarian conferences. Gradually I began speaking at these conferences on the need for economic freedom in Africa. But I realized that while the libertarians welcomed my message on the need for economic freedom in Africa, only some of them were inspired to work toward prosperity for Africa. (For me, and for Michael, "liberty" was never the cause. Prosperity—and the ensuing dignity—for Africa was always the cause).

A very special balm for my heart at this time was the work of economist George Ayittey, starting with his book *Africa Unchained*. While my beloved professor (I can't help but think of him that way) provides abundant information on how foreign aid has damaged Africa and why greater economic freedom is needed in Africa, that is not what touched me. What touched me in his work was the simple insight that from its earliest days Africa was a market society. At the most basic level, the traditional marketplace was the centerpiece of African society. In some respects it is the beating heart of the matriarchy of Africa.

Every African village has a marketplace, and all the sellers are women.

It is worth remembering just how anti-capitalist the mainstream establishment was in the 1960s and 1970s in order to appreciate George's achievement in understanding the need for economic freedom in Africa. Marxists dominated much of academia in the 1950s, '60s, and '70s. Pol Pot and his fellow Khmer Rouge intellectuals received their Marxist education at elite French institutions in the 1950s. Leopold Senghor, the first president of independent Senegal, was a socialist. There were many more.

The first four Pan-African Congresses were organized by W.E.B. DuBois, an African American socialist intellectual. The fifth Pan-African Congress, held in 1945 just after WWII, crystallized the role that modern African socialism came to play in the coming independence movement. In addition to DuBois, who was older at this point, prominent attendees included Jomo Kenyatta, Kwame Nkrumah, and Hastings Banda, the first leaders of independent Kenya, Ghana, and Malawi, respectively. The conference attendees were united in calling for African independence from colonial powers.

One of the great tragedies of twentieth-century Africa is that "socialism" was associated with anti-colonialism, whereas "capitalism" was believed to be imperialist—and therefore colonialist by nature. Lenin originally made this argument early in the twentieth century; by 1945, most intellectuals still believed it. The Soviet Union had been partially discredited by the show trials of the late 1930s and, even worse, by Stalin's alliance with

Hitler. But most Western and African intellectuals still wanted to believe that socialism was fundamentally sound and that Stalin had simply perverted Lenin's dream.

Marxist socialism was gospel among African intellectuals of the time. After the fifth Pan-African Congress, Kwame Nkrumah began promoting the idea of a "Union of Socialist States" in Africa using the Soviet Union as a model. Eric Coffie, founder and president of the Economic Freedom Institute in Ghana, wrote:

Kwame Nkrumah became prime minister of Ghana and later president of the new republic in 1960. He was the winner of the Lenin Peace Prize in 1962. Nkrumah founded numerous state-run companies, launched the construction of a huge dam for the generation of hydroelectric power, built schools and universities, and backed liberation movements in African colonies that had yet to achieve independence.

In 1964, faced with economic crises caused largely by his Marxist economic policies, Nkrumah's proposed solution was to tighten government control. He declared Ghana a one-party communist state with himself as president for life. Nkrumah was accused of actively promoting a cult of personality (Nkrumahism), which eventually led to his overthrow in 1966 by military coup d'état. He died in Bucharest, Romania, after six years in exile in Guinea, at age sixty-two. In the year 2000, Nkrumah was voted Africa's "Man of the Millennium" by BBC listeners as a "Hero of Independence" and an "international symbol of freedom as the leader of the first African country to shake off the chains of colonial rule."[4]

---

4 Eric Coffie, "Marxism in Africa: Why So Many African Economies Failed after Independence," *Mises Wire*, November 4, 2020, https://mises.org/wire/marxism-africa-why-so-many-african-economies-failed-after-independence.

How are we to think about all the socialist African leaders today? Are we really supposed to regard them as "international symbols of freedom"? I do believe most of these men were genuinely motivated by the noble intention to build a free Africa. But the results speak for themselves.

This is a hard problem because on the one hand, they do deserve immense credit for shaking off the chains of colonial rule. Moreover, as individuals they are hardly to blame for the fact that their intellectual milieu regarded Marxist socialism as a credible political and economic perspective. In 1945, at the fifth Pan-African Congress, when the future of socialist Africa was established, it was widely believed that the Soviet Union, despite Stalin's excesses, was a successful model of economic development. George Padmore, a Black Caribbean activist who was, with Nkrumah, key to organizing the 1945 conference, said:

I tell all the young Africans, read Marx, Lenin, Trotsky and all of them, to see what you can learn from them about freeing your country. And because they're White don't dismiss them, 'cause ideas don't know any color line. Study the way the Communist Party organizes, they are great organizers... Next, study the Soviet Union, because you're going to have to develop your country. Those people learned how to develop a country so fast that they stood up to Hitler—find out how they did it. But your job is to deal with Africa and don't let them lead you astray by saying someday the European proletariat is going to lay down its tools in order to free colonials—they ain't going to do it. But I'll tell you what could happen—someday you may get strong enough so that if you pull Africa out of the imperial structure you'll force those workers up there to go left and build socialism in their own country.[5]

Even into the 1960s and '70s many continued to believe that the Soviet Union was a functioning model. As Peter Dwyer, from Ruskin College, Oxford, and Leo Zeilig, editor of the *Review of African Political Economy*, put it in 2018:

> For much of the century the ideas of Marxism were seemingly omnipotent in Africa. They dominated every serious intellectual debate about the continent and occupied the minds of those who sought independence. It was assumed by many anti-colonial leaders that poverty and underdevelopment would only be reversed by the application of socialism, or more specifically the Soviet model of economic development.[6]

In the 1950s, '60s, and into the '70s it was widely believed that Mao had also created a successful model of socialism. J. K. Gailbraith's 1973 book, *A China Passage*, claimed that Mao's model worked, even as he downplayed claims about the Cultural Revolution. Many intellectuals supported socialism until its unexpected collapse in 1989.

What immense damage these misguided leaders caused! Not only did they further impoverish Africa through government-controlled economies, but they also established one-party dictatorial

---

5 George Shepperson and St. Clair Drake, "The Fifth Pan-African Conference, 1945 and the All African People's Congress, 1958," *Contributions in Black Studies* vol 8, article 5 (2008): 21, https://scholarworks.umass.edu/cibs/vol8/iss1/5.

6 Peter Dwyer and Leo Zeilig, "Marxism, class and revolution in Africa: the legacy of the 1917 Russian Revolution," *International Socialism*, January 9, 2018, http://isj.org.uk/marxism-class-and-revolution-in-africa-the-legacy-of-the-1917-russian-revolution.

states across Africa. Is all of this due to socialist beliefs and policies? No, but much of it is.

For Africa to move forward, we must solidly and uniformly repudiate the dreadful socialist legacy of our founding fathers. We should regard them as tragic figures, beholden to false and harmful ideas. We can honor them for moving forward toward independence with noble intentions, but their fatal flaws must be acknowledged.

In addition to Nkrumah, other founding fathers included Julius Nyerere of Tanzania, Kenneth Kaunda of Zambia, Leopold Senghor of Senegal, Modiba Keita of Mali, Mathieu Kerekou of Benin, and Sekou Toure of Guinea. Senghor, to his credit, advocated for a non-Marxist version of socialism.

Full-on Marxist-Leninist communist states in Africa included:

- People's Republic of the Congo (1969–92)
- Somali Democratic Republic (1969–91)
- Provisional Military Government of Socialist Ethiopia (1974–87)
- People's Democratic Republic of Ethiopia (1987–91)
- People's Republic of Mozambique (1975–90)
- People's Republic of Angola (1975–92)
- People's Republic of Benin (1975–90)
- People's Republic of Burkina Faso (1984–87)

Also socialist but not specifically Marxist-Leninist regimes in Africa included Cape Verde (1975–92), Chad (1962–75), Republic of Congo (1963–68), Djibouti (1981–92), Egypt (1953–2007), Equatorial Guinea (1970–79), Guinea (1958–84), Libya (1969–2011), Madagascar (1975–92), Mali (1960–91), Mauritania (1961–78), Senegal (1960–81), Seychelles (1977–91), Sierra Leone (1978–91), Sudan (1969–85), Tunisia (1964–88), and Zambia (1973–91).

Note the wave of collapses in the early 1990s. As the Soviet Union and its associated support and prestige vanished, most Marxist and non-Marxist socialist states vanished. Other avowedly socialist nations to this day in Africa include Algeria, Eritrea, Guinea-Bissau, and Sahrawi (claiming a portion of "western Morocco"). All continue to claim to be socialist.

Even this list understates the extent to which postcolonial Africa was influenced by socialist ideas. For instance, while it is true that in 1981 Senegal legalized non-socialist political parties, Senghor's handpicked socialist successor was president until 2000, thus making Senegal de facto socialist from 1960 to 2000. Separately, while Nigeria was one of the few African nations that didn't start out as an explicitly socialist nation, several of the leading figures in the early Nigerian postcolonial regime were socialists. Indeed, postcolonial so-called capitalist Nigeria included Soviet-style "Five year plans" for the economy. It was "capitalism" from a heavily state-led perspective.

Then, of course, there are other figures, such as Robert Mugabe, leader of Zimbabwe (1980–2017), who claimed to be socialist and was widely supported in his early days as yet another African socialist revolutionary. Later, Bishop Desmond Tutu was to describe him as "a cartoon figure of an archetypal African dictator."

(Here's a revealing popular joke: "Of course we have democracy in Africa. One man, one vote, one time"—indicating no subsequent elections.)

In Senegal, Senghor had been lionized as a great figure. How could I question our founding father? On the other hand, he put Cheihk Anta Diop, our leading intellectual, in prison early on for starting a competing political party. Later on, his hand-picked socialist successor, Abdou Diouf, also put Abdoulaye Wade, president of Senegal from 2000 to 2012, in prison several times, largely for being part of the political opposition. I knew these facts about him before I began questioning the anti-capitalist beliefs of my friends in San Francisco.

But after I began to understand the need for economic freedom in Africa, I realized that I would need to reevaluate the legendary founding generation of independence leaders. This is a reckoning that all Africans must do in order to discover a clear path forward for Africa.

George Ayittey had his eyes opened to the unnatural and ahistorical role of socialism in Africa by his love and respect for market women (like his own mother), whom he saw abused. When he began speaking and writing about the issue in the late 1970s and early 1980s, he was among a handful of global thinkers who believed that free markets were a more effective path to development. As George put it in *Africa Unchained*:

> Markets were not invented by Europeans and transplanted into Africa. There were free village markets in Africa before the Europeans stepped foot on the continent. This is not a veiled attempt to rewrite history but a statement of fact. Timbuktu, Salaga, Kano, and Mombasa were all great market towns of yesteryear. It is rather bizarre and an act of unpardonable cultural sabotage for African governments to pursue strident anti-market policies. For example, rural market activity in Africa has always been dominated by women, and these women traders have always been free enterprisers. Free trade routes crisscrossed the continent even centuries before the arrival of the Europeans. Free village markets, free enterprise, and free trade are part and parcel of Africa's indigenous economic heritage. These constitute the "roots" upon which the future of Africa must be built.[7]

---

7 George B.N. Ayittey, *Africa Unchained* (New York: Palgrave Macmillan 2005), 31.

In addition to his recognition that African cultures are fundamentally pro-market, George also reminded the world that traditional African cultures would never let their leaders abuse their people as the one-party socialist revolutionaries abused theirs.

As George notes, traditional African leaders would have never interfered with the standard buying and selling in a marketplace the way that socialist African leaders routinely did. Moreover, many tribes could and did regularly depose abusive leaders. Or dissatisfied members of a tribe could break off and form their own new community.

An article on Botswana's traditions highlights the deference that traditional leaders had for the people:

A Setswana saying conveys an important attribute of traditional culture: "Kgosi ke Kgosi ka batho": a chief is a chief by the will of the people. Chiefs generally consulted people before making a decision on matters of any importance. While they did not necessarily abide by the consensus of opinion in the *kgotla,* the tradition of consultation and seeking consensus is deeply important in Tswana society. A chief would seldom venture an opinion in the *kgotla* until all who wished to opine had done so.[8]

None of the postcolonial leaders who used state force to keep themselves in power demonstrated this traditional respect for and deference to the people.

From this perspective, the entire state apparatus of colonialism was leveraged, using the goal of independence to create abusive leaders the likes of which traditional Africa had never seen. Mugabe was strictly a monster of the state. If we Africans

---

8 Stephen R. Lewis Jr., "Explaining Botswana's Success: The Importance of Culture," Carleton College, last modified June 18, 2020, https://www.carleton.edu/president/lewis/speeches-writings/botswana-success/.

really want to return to our roots, we should not only question the socialist regimes installed by most leaders at independence, but we should also question the entire monopoly of governance provided by the modern state.

And why should we not question the legacy of our former colonial masters?

For much of the twentieth century, the assumption among scholars was that African society had long been organized in patterns that were similar to those of socialist and communist societies. This was made possible by the lack of documented evidence, which was scant, and even more so following the cultural destruction pursued by the colonial powers. As Ibrahim Anoba wrote on AfricanLiberty.org:

> They historically presented the collective purpose against individual purpose by arguing the true and only philosophy in traditional Africa was the philosophy of brotherhood and welfarism, which prevented anyone from becoming more prosperous than everyone else. They rejected all notions of self-determinism or personal ambition as non-existential in traditional Africa while claiming a strongman leadership of interest was the choice of governance in the most part of African political history.[9]

"Strongman leadership" as the natural order in Africa. Convenient, right? But as Anoba points out, new scholarship proves that the "strongman" style of postcolonial African leaders is *not* the indigenous leadership model of all African communities:

---

9 Ibrahim Anoba, "Communism in Africa: Errors in Early Literature," African Liberty, October 22, 2018, https://www.africanliberty.org/2018/10/22/africas-communist-foundations-2/.

In some early African communities authority was not central, while in others, they never even existed. In some cases, people were entitled to self-determinism under anarchic and acephalous communities. Some even had well-organized administrative structures without monarchs or a centralized ruling elite council.

In communities like the *Tallensi* (Ghana), *Logoli* (Kenya) and *Nuer* (South Sudan) there were no institutions that regulated social life but were purely anarchic. In communities with clearly defined systems of governance, the majority of them had structures for institutional ombudsman and separation of powers among governing councils—comparable to the tripartite system proposed by French philosopher Baron de Montesquieu in *The Spirit of the Laws* (1748).

These communities also treasured standards for checks and balances to avoid power concentration or abuse by an individual or group. For example, in the *Igbo* community (Nigeria), authority was shared among groups like the *ofo* (family heads), *ozo* (nobles) and the age-grade groups with similar model among the *Yoruba* (Nigeria), the *Bété*, *Dida* and *Baoulé* (Côte d'Ivoire), the *Nuer* and *Dinka Gnoc* (South Sudan), the *Massai* (Kenya), the *Nyjakusa* (Tanzania) and *Tonga* (Zambia) tribes.[10]

The monolithic state that came to dominate postcolonial nations is strictly a colonial import—and a tragic one.

More intriguingly, at least some African societies had been able to develop sophisticated governance structures without a state at all. While Somalia since 1992 has been regarded as a byword for anarchy, there is a long-standing but little known debate regarding the extent to which indigenous Somali legal

---

10 Anoba, "Communism in Africa."

and governance structures have given Somalia certain advantages. Without going into all the debates, the short version is that *kritarchy*, the rule of judges from traditional Somali clans, successfully replaced government in many parts of the region. The anthropologist Spencer MacCallum has made the case that the egregious violence in the Mogadishu area has been due to the fact that the international community forced an unwelcome and unnatural central government on the Somalis. By doing so, they created high-stakes incentives for inter-clan battles for supremacy, including a lawful monopoly on force and significant foreign aid.

Moreover, the difficulties Somalia has had since 1992 have been little different from those of many other African nations since the collapse of the Soviet empire. Civil wars in Africa since 1989 include violence in Liberia, Rwanda, Niger, Mali, Djibouti, Sierra Leone, Algeria, Somalia, Burundi, Congo, Namibia, Ethiopia, Uganda, Eritrea, Guinea-Bissau, Ivory Coast, Central African Republic, Sudan, Chad, Kenya, Cameroon, Comoros, South Sudan, and Libya.[11]

Indeed, although the definition of conflict varies, it has been credibly claimed that the only two sub-Saharan African nations to have avoided coups and civil wars since their independence are Senegal and Botswana.

Almost anyone familiar with the history of civil conflict in Africa realizes that the artificial boundaries imposed by colonial powers do not align with the ethnic realities on the ground. By means of organizing Africans from the outside into nation-states with arbitrarily drawn boundaries ruled by a central government, the West recklessly created a staging ground for ethnic conflict. Minority ethnicities are generally concerned that they will be abused by those who capture the power of the central government.

---

[11] Meredith Reid Sarkees and Frank Wayman, *Resort to War: 1816–2007* (Washington DC: CQ Press, 2010), https://correlatesofwar.org/data-sets/COW-war.

Therefore, they are all too easily prone to be organized either to join separatist movements or to engage in conflict in order to achieve their goals. The exact same dynamic resulted in the post-Marxist breakdown of Yugoslavia into five different countries, with similar violence between ethnic enclaves.

This is not the place to go into how to address those challenges. But I do want to remind my fellow Africans and the world that:

Our indigenous institutions were entirely supportive of voluntary market transactions (a.k.a. "capitalism"). These market institutions led to various wealthy African empires over the centuries. In some periods, various African empires were wealthier than European nations of the same time.

The Marxist state socialism of our leaders at independence was profoundly un-African. In every nation where it was imposed, the result was poverty and violence.

The nation-states of Africa today are themselves a residue of colonialism and are unnatural. They contain within themselves the seeds of endless conflict.

◇◇◇◇◇◇◇◇◇◇◇◇◇◇

As we take back our heritage from the West, we need to examine and reexamine which Western institutions are aligned with our indigenous institutions and with our best future interests—and which are not.

Finally, just a few words about Senegal and Botswana, the two outliers with respect to civil conflict. My country, Senegal, has avoided conflict largely due to the influence of the Sufi brotherhoods, which are committed to peace. For example, Cheikh Ahmadou Bamba, the founder of Mouridism, the largest and most influential of the primary four Sufi brotherhoods, was a principled advocate of nonviolence in the late nineteenth century, well before Tolstoy, Gandhi, or Martin Luther King Jr. became famous for promoting nonviolence.

Anthropologists and political scientists have studied the role of the Sufi brotherhoods in quelling hot-headed young men who might otherwise be prone to violence—as are hot-headed young men everywhere around the world.

"One of the defining features of postcolonial Senegalese political life was the embrace of Sufi orders and religious leaders (Marabouts) by the country's first president, Leopold Senghor, even though Senghor was Catholic,"[12] wrote West African scholar Andrew Lebovich. Senghor made many mistakes, but his respect for the traditional Sufi brotherhoods has paid massive dividends.

Botswana had the good fortune to have as its first post-independence leader Seretse Khama, who was both lineage royalty in his nation and an Oxford-educated lawyer. Khama wisely integrated the best of his nation's traditional legal system with British common law. As one article notes:

> The BDP [Botswana Democratic Party] had studied other constitutions before drafting their own proposals for the constitutional conference...
>
> The BDP leaders searched for a "golden mean" on the role of chiefs and of customary laws and practices...
>
> Chiefs retained their roles as adjudicators of disputes and dispensers of justice according to customary law. Thus, for the average citizen, the legal system would not change after independence. An appeals court ensured congruence among customary, statute and common law, and also provided

---

12 Shadi Hamid and Andrew Lebovich, "Why are there so few Islamists in West Africa? A dialogue between Shadi Hamid and Andrew Lebovich," The Brookings Institution, April 20, 2017, https://www.brookings.edu/on-the-record/why-are-there- so-few-islamists-in-west-africa-a-dialogue-between-shadi-hamid-and-andrew-lebovich/.

uniformity in the application of the law and a forum for appeal. Customary courts were established in urban areas and the new mining towns, so that both urban and rural Batswanans [sic] could bring cases for adjudication without a lawyer. Today, 75 to 80 percent of all civil and minor criminal cases are still settled in customary courts.

The reform of chieftainship was doubtless eased by the fact that Seretse Khama was of royal heritage...

The strong Tswana tradition of consultation was embraced by the BDP leader. It influenced how they recruited party members, how they approached the electorate, and how they formulated policy and made decisions. The *kgotla* tradition of people speaking their minds candidly was easily transferable to a system of democratic elections with a bill of rights that protects freedom of speech and encourages widespread consultation.[13]

The thoughtful integration of traditional customary law and British common law provided Botswana with a uniquely sound legal foundation. As a result, from 1960 to 1980, Botswana was the fastest-growing nation in the world. To this day Botswana is ranked in the top five best-governed nations in Africa on the Ibrahim Index of African Governance (2019), and Senegal is in the top ten.[14] Note what both of these exceptions have in common: a foundation based on precolonial indigenous institutions—in the case of Senegal, the Sufi brotherhoods; in the case of

---

13 Stephen R. Lewis Jr., "Explaining Botswana's Success: The Importance of Culture," Carleton College, last modified June 18, 2020, https://www.carleton.edu/president/lewis/speeches-writings/botswana-success/.

14 Mo Ibrahim Foundation, *2020 Ibrahim Index of African Governance Index Report*, 2020, https://mo.ibrahim.foundation/sites/default/files/2020-11/2020-index-report.pdf.

Botswana, traditional Botswanan customary law complemented by British common law.

If only other postcolonial African nations had similarly respected their customary laws and market relationships instead of forcing an alien socialist state onto their peoples!

CHAPTER NINE

Àkk àkkum gaynde, song songum bukki. (Charge with
the spirit of a lion, but attack like a hyena.)

◇◇◇◇◇◇◇◇◇◇◇◇◇◇◇

S OMETIMES I BECOME VERY DISCOURAGED. But
when I do, I always recall one day in 2007 when I watched
Africa's possible future open up right before my eyes.

I was in Arusha, Tanzania, at a meeting of TED Global. TED
is a nonprofit that promotes new ideas by hosting meetings where
various speakers give "short, powerful talks." It's proved to be
an amazingly popular program, with the videos of these talks
drawing tens of millions of views on YouTube.

I was there as one of one hundred Africans who had been
chosen to join the first cohort of TED Fellows. At the time, Africa
was a trendy topic among the world's intelligentsia, and TED was
hip. Everybody who was anybody was there, including Bill Gates,
the Google boys, and even Bono, the lead singer of U2.

It was to these sophisticates that George Ayittey spoke his
mind. What a revelation! He was on fire. George first thanked
TED for putting together what he called the most important
conference of the twenty-first century. And then he made it so.

He referred to us TED Fellows as the "Cheetah Generation"
(and thereby gave this book and my new initiative their titles).

He defined us as "a new breed who brook no nonsense about corruption. They understand what accountability and democracy is…they're not going to wait for the government to do things for them. Africa's salvation rests on their backs."

This was the call to action we had been waiting for. It was electrifying for the one hundred fellows, but it also had a profound impact on all the do-gooders crowded into the room. It was the first time many had heard George's ideas, the indispensable ideas that will lift Africa out of poverty. First and foremost, of course, that means Africans must lift ourselves. We can't rely on what George mockingly called the "Hippo Generation"—the ruling elites.

What did Africa's ruling elites want? More foreign aid, of course. Why? Because they steal it.

Finally, here was a man telling the aid cartel the ugly truth. Not only was the aid they were throwing at Africa not helping common Africans, but it was propping up some of the worst people on the continent. They were shocked.

George was giving it to them with both barrels.

"The ruling elites are stuck in their intellectual patch, complaining about colonialism and imperialism," he said. "If you ask them to reform their economies, they're not going to reform it because they benefit from the rotten status quo."

It was thrilling, not least because if you had asked most of those in attendance why Africa was poor, the first words out of their mouths would have been colonialism and imperialism. But here was George telling them they had it all wrong. "Helping Africa is noble," he said, "but helping Africa is like a theater of the absurd. It's like the blind leading the clueless."

And as for the leaders of Africa? "If you look at the slate of post-colonial African leaders," he said, you will see "an assortment of military fufu heads, Swiss bank socialists, crocodile liberators, vampire elites, [and] quack liberators! In Africa the governments are the problem!"

Is it any wonder I was so jazzed?

And then came Andrew Mwenda, who picked up where George left off. Mwenda spoke directly to those in attendance, pointing out that at the same time the TED conference was being held, the G-8 was meeting in Berlin. The leaders of the eight largest economies in the world have a solution to African poverty, he said: a massive increase in aid.

Mwenda called it nonsense.

He said the world sees Africa wrongly because the media plays up its worst difficulties, from civil war to famine. Africa is much more, he said, and the real problems are much different. Yes, donated medicines are helpful, and so are peacekeeping troops. But those who seek to help must provide aid in a way that doesn't reduce initiative.

That means, Mwenda said, the "international aid cartel" must revise its priorities. Instead of seeking poverty reduction, they should be promoting wealth creation.

"Treating the symptoms is not productive," he said. "Where does wealth come from? Entrepreneurs. So where should we be putting the money? We need to put it where it can productively grow!"

Support private investment in Africa!

I wanted to stand up and cheer, so I did.

And then something funny happened. Mwenda asked if anyone could name a person who had become wealthy by receiving charity. Silence. He followed that up with another question: "Do any of you know of a country that grew wealthy because of the kindness and generosity of another?"

The audience was again dead silent for a few seconds, but then we heard a voice shouting in the audience. "Yes," cried Bono. "Ireland!"

Mwenda corrected Bono gently, saying that Ireland had been given an opportunity, not wealth. "You have to take up the opportunities yourself."

And then he added, "Africa has received many opportunities but has done nothing with them. Why? Because Africa has a poor institutional and policy framework." He pointed out that most governments—those in the rest of the world—must raise the needed revenues from the population. A healthy tax base requires healthy businesses and individuals. In most of the world, the leadership can't completely undermine those who are creating wealth.

But in Africa, Mwenda said, we don't do that. Our incentives are distorted by aid.

African governments can and do ignore their people and instead endlessly negotiate with the International Monetary Fund, the World Bank, and the cartel of do-gooders in the world. (More recently China has been added to the mix—and Chinese funding doesn't even pretend to promote human rights.)

What he was kind enough not to say was nevertheless heard loud and clear by those in the audience: "They can just ask you for the money."

Because the government has essentially all the money, the most ambitious always seek a toehold. The result is ludicrous. In his home nation of Uganda, Mwenda said, the president had 114 official advisors "who only see him on TV."

The aid money continues to pour in, but it has no effect on poverty. Where does it go? A recent government study, Mwenda said, revealed the Ugandan Ministry of Health had three thousand four-wheel drive vehicles at its headquarters. Uganda has 916 sub-counties, he added, each with a dispensary. Not one has an ambulance.

The four-wheel drive vehicles are at the headquarters "to drive around the ministers, the permanent secretaries, the bureaucrats, and the international aid bureaucrats who work in aid projects, while the poor die without medicines and ambulances."

Oh, what an uproar! What a marvelous event!

George has compiled lists of the dictators and how much wealth they've accumulated, which is often in the hundreds of millions or even billions of dollars. In his words:

When Angola's socialist president, Jose Eduardo dos Santos, stepped down after 39 years in power in 2017, he had accumulated a net worth of $20 billion. His daughter, Isabel, is Africa's richest woman, checking in with a net worth of $2.2 billion. Meanwhile, 60 percent of Angolans live on less than $2 a day—the very definition of poverty. Some socialists!

Other African leaders also betrayed the cause of freedom by capturing the state and transforming the presidency into their family property. "Government" disappeared—hijacked by a phalanx of bandits, crooks, and gangsters who used the state machinery to enrich themselves, cronies, and tribesmen, excluding everybody else. The richest are heads of state and ministers. Quite often, the chief bandit is the head of state himself. For context, consider that the net worth of 43 U.S. presidents—from Washington to Obama—amounted to $2.7 billion in 2010 dollars. By contrast, the following African presidents—Abacha, Babangida, Bashir, Mubarak, and Mobutu—*each* stole more than the net worth of 43 U.S. presidents *combined!*

That style of governance is alien. Traditional African chiefs do not brutalize their people, loot the tribal treasury for deposit in foreign banks, and remain chiefs while their people suffer in misery.[15]

◇◇◇◇◇◇◇◇◇◇◇◇◇

George gave Bono a copy of his book, *Africa Unchained*, the book that changed everything for me and will eventually do the same for all of Africa.

I give Bono a lot more credit than most. Seven years later he had come around and had begun calling aid a "stopgap" effort. He even promoted the idea, which I agree with, that "trade is better than aid." Perhaps most notably, he has created a company that buys goods made in Africa and resells them in the United States and Europe.

TED organized another conference ten years later. Bono wasn't there, of course. Nor were the Google boys or Bill Gates. In the intervening years Africa had lost its cachet. Nonetheless, I was happy to see my friends, though Mwenda was missing. We thought maybe he was in jail again, which is where he has spent a good deal of his time these last years due to his outspoken opposition to the government. But the world's charities had moved on to other issues, not the least of which was the 2008 economic crisis.

In the United States, a series of Black people being shot by the police, starting with Michael Brown in 2014 in Ferguson, Missouri, also refocused the US population on their own racial issues.

That said, the extent to which Africa is no longer on the awareness radar of do-gooders in the West is still surprising to me. I can't help but wonder if Africa was more exciting when we were regarded as hopeless pity cases than when we began to be regarded as entrepreneurs and change agents in our own right.

---

15 George B.N. Aittey, Take Back Africa!, https://www.patreon.com/user?u=29211917.

BONO AND GEORGE AYITTEY

CHAPTER TEN

Xam-xam ñeent a koy kulóor: di ko bind, di ko jàngale, di ko waxtaane, mbaa di ko. (There are four things to do with knowledge: write it, teach it, talk about it, and do it.)

◇◇◇◇◇◇◇◇◇◇◇◇◇◇

T HE TIMING OF THAT FIRST TED GLOBAL CONFERENCE in Tanzania in 2007 worked out well for me, and not just because I was already engaged in questioning everything I thought I knew about poverty and the creation of wealth. As it happens, I was also being asked on regular occasions to speak to similar audiences, particularly at universities. My speaking career began because of Adina. When I started Adina I was arguably one of the first Africans to do what I did. Before me, many White people had brought indigenous recipes, reformulated and rebranded, to the Whole Foods demographic. But I was one of the first Africans to bring something from my homeland.

Certainly my message on branding resonated for audiences in the developing world.

You must understand: the dominance of US culture around the world is overwhelming. The motivation that led me to launch Adina—my dismay at watching my culture disappear in the face of US and other Western brands—is happening everywhere. US commercial brands, thanks to the internet and globalization, are gaining market share against local indigenous products and associated cultural traditions around the world.

That's why many people from developing nations—even among the educated and well traveled—were unaware of the appetite in the United States for culturally authentic brands from elsewhere. When I spoke in my talks about the power of branding one's own indigenous products as both a way to make money and to support one's own culture, audiences in Africa, the Middle East, and Latin America sat up and listened. After my talks, aspiring young entrepreneurs would invariably come up and discuss their ideas for packaging their culture's products for Western customers.

In a world that was divided between artists and cultural creatives on the one hand and hard-nosed ambitious business people on the other, I provided an interesting new perspective. I was personally very impressed with the power of consumer brands. Everywhere I went young people were totally focused on US consumer brands: Levi's, Apple, and more. Everyone wants to go to Disney World. When I pointed this out to my international audience, they sheepishly acknowledged that, yes, their minds are dominated by US brands. I then explained that even the iconic figure of Santa Claus with a long white beard, round belly, cheerful demeanor, and a bright red suit is the legacy of a Coca-Cola marketing campaign from the 1930s. Yet now around the world that is the image everyone has of Santa Claus.

Since I launched Adina and then Tiossan, many more African brands have been developed. These days I see House of Tayo, Bantu Wax, Mami Wata, Sole Rebels, Alaffia, and many others. There has been a small revolution of African brands. But when I started Adina, my fellow Africans laughed at me. Few believed it could be done. It makes me proud that I opened a breach into the West, and many have followed me.

I had two big breaks that established my larger draw as a speaker. The first was the Global Competitiveness Forum in Riyadh in 2009. At the time I was a staunch organic fair-trade person, tooth-and-tong opposed to what I considered back then to be massive evil corporations.

When I received my invitation and saw the list of speakers, I first thought there was a mistake in my being invited. The list was full of titles like CEO of Airbus, chairman of Goldman Sachs, CEO of 3M, former prime minister of Canada, former prime minister of Great Britain, and so on and so forth. And then me: Magatte Wade, this very young woman, barely out of my twenties, president of a small company. I remember turning to Michael and saying, "Could they not find a better African token? This is ridiculous!"

Fortunately, he knew what to say. "I don't think that's what's going on. You need to give yourself more credit. And even if it is, you will show them that you earned your presence there."

I liked that!

Then I learned I was not just to speak but to debate Peter Brabeck-Letmathe, the chairman and former CEO of Nestle. We would argue about the importance of organics. Brabeck-Letmathe was arguing against organics; I was arguing for. It turned out the conference organizer was 100 percent sold on my commitment to sustainability.

Not to worry. I rose to the stage full of confidence. After all, I had nothing but disdain for Nestle and most of their practices. I immediately took the fight to Brabeck-Letmathe. During one heated moment, and in front of that crowd of several hundred of the world's leading movers and shakers, I turned and pointed to him and said, "I believe in criticizing by creating. You are one of the reasons that I created Adina." Oh, the crowd loved that, and it put him on the defensive from that point on.

In fact, I was doing very well until our moderator, Riz Khan (a prominent BBC, CNN, and Al Jazeera journalist), asked me the question that almost ruined everything. He asked a minute-long very technical question about water. Because of its importance to the company's bottom line, water is one of Brabeck-Letmathe's specialties.

Ouch. Michael had wanted to prep me on the topic, but I had brushed it off because I found it too technical. Poor Michael, he was listening on Skype. He was cringing, but there was nothing he could do for me at that particular moment.

As Khan was finally finishing his question, I realized I had no viable answer. I had a horrible feeling of disappointment growing in me. I thought I had finally been caught and it was revealed that I had no business being there in the first place. The fact that I had no relevant answer to this question was the proof. Big swollen tears started to form, and as I was getting ready to get up and leave the stage crying, the miracle happened. Brabeck-Letmathe, who had been stung by what I told him earlier, lost his manners and did not let me answer the question but instead began defending himself from my earlier attack. Khan tried, as a gentleman, to give me a chance to answer his question, but then the same thing happened again. I just told him, "It's okay, Riz! Let's move on."

From there, I just picked up the ball and pulled the audience back onto my turf, one that I knew I controlled very well because organics and sustainability is something I live for and believe in to my core. Brabeck was so mad he blurted out, "Organics is just a marketing gimmick!"

Wow! This from the man who had declared that his chairmanship would reflect a new goal of "organic and fair trade."

So I won the debate, and people began to take notice. The Saudis responded particularly well. I was a regular speaker at that conference for the next several years. I also received invitations to speak at several Saudi women's universities, along with conferences in Dubai and, eventually, around the world. A lot of people in developing countries liked me. Even today in the United States, high school girls and young women identify with me. They see a strong woman.

The second big break was the article Michael and I wrote about Jeff Sachs in the *Huffington Post*—the one that erupted after I read the Millennium Villages brochure that warned visitors not to feed the natives. I already had a reputation as someone with different ideas about Africa. I didn't want the aid, and I particularly didn't want the condescension. That was a novel take on aid. It didn't hurt that I was going after one of the "golden boys."

Since then, I've been in demand. I've never signed up for a speaking bureau because I don't need to. I get more invitations than I can handle as it is. At the same time, the core of my message has slowly shifted from branding and organics to the greater importance of improving the African business environment. I am still passionate about my branding work and still an advocate of doing business in a way that does not harm the environment. But bringing a billion-plus Africans out of poverty is the much greater cause.

Just as my friendship network shifted from progressive to libertarian, my speaking opportunities and audiences changed as well. I noticed I was getting more interest from the libertarian movement. That started with the Universidad Francisco Marroquín, the heroic college in Guatemala City. And then the Foundation for Economic Education (FEE) in the United States latched on. I've spoken to the Mt. Pelerin Society and the Cato Institute and been on John Stossel's show.

But regardless of my audience and its leaning, my message remains the same: if we want Africans to prosper, we need to work toward greater economic freedom in Africa.

George Scharffenberger, a scion of the chocolate company from San Francisco, continues to invite me to speak at Berkeley, where he teaches part time. He was part of my circle before my conversion and, remarkably, he's still a good friend. He's an honest, decent person who likes the green, fair trade ideas but also recognizes the value of free markets and social enterprise. He doesn't like to shout about it but has always provided his support in spreading my message.

Let me pause for a moment.

Dear reader, can you hear this? Do you understand what this message means?

- In the Central African Republic, it takes 17 documents, 55 days, and US$5,555 per container to import goods.
- In Angola, you must undertake 44 procedures requiring 1,296 days to enforce a contract. On average the process will cost 44 percent of the claim.
- In Eritrea, it takes 13 procedures, 84 days, and 21 percent of the average income per capita, along with 94 percent of average income per capita in paid-in capital, to start a legal business. (An Eritrean basically has to deposit a year's income in order to start a legal business).

Compare that to New Zealand, where starting a business requires one procedure, half a day, with 0.2 percent of average income per capita. And there is no minimum capital requirement.

My home country of Senegal is much better than Eritrea, thanks to reforms in recent years. It now takes four procedures, six days, 23 percent of average income per capita, and 3 percent of average income per capita in paid-in capital.

There are a few African nations in the top half of the World Bank's Doing Business (DB) index (ranking out of 190 countries):

13: Mauritius (a small island nation that is now middle income thanks to its business environment)

38: Rwanda (in recent years a top improver on DB rankings of the World Bank and often the fastest-growing economy in Africa)

56: Kenya (go Kenya!)

84: South Africa (sadly falling on Doing Business rankings)

85: Zambia (barely in the top half, but still good)

87: Botswana (barely in the top half, but still good)

Meanwhile, look at the bottom twenty:

171: Sudan (Africa)

172: Iraq (war)

173: Afghanistan (war)

174: Guinea-Bissau (Africa)

175: Liberia (Africa)

176: Syria (war)

177: Angola (Africa)

178: Equatorial Guinea (Africa)

179: Haiti (renowned basket case)

180: Republic of Congo (Africa)

181: Timor-Leste (war)

182: Chad (Africa)

183: Dem. Republic of Congo (Africa)

184: Central African Republic (Africa)

185: South Sudan (Africa)

186: Libya (renowned basket case)

187: Yemen (war)

188: Venezuela (renowned basket case)

189: Eritrea (Africa)

190: Somalia (Africa)

Could it be any more obvious?

Let's talk about the result of this paperwork mess. Many people skip right past all this hassle of paperwork to start a business through the age-old, tried-and-true method: they bribe the officials.

People always talk about how much corruption there is in Africa. It's another very true strike against us. But people talk about corruption as if it's a root problem. They believe that African people are inherently more prone to corruption than others. But that isn't the case.

Corruption is a natural consequence of too many senseless laws—laws that keep us poor.

Would there be as much corruption in the United States if contractors had to deal with truckloads of regulations just to build a house? You bet. I have many US friends who share privately the names of construction workers who will work without permits. They pay a premium for them!

In Africa, and in the United States, the only way to fix corruption is by reducing and simplifying the laws.

The good news is that my country, Senegal, has been working hard to streamline the process of starting a business. The bad news? Well, let's look at a few features of the "streamlined" version provided by the Agence de Promotion de l'Investissement et des Grands Travaux (APIX), our "one-stop shop" for business startups.

It is possible to apply for an exemption from paying taxes on labor and equipment for the first three years of operations (with a possibility of extending it another two years). This is called the investment period. This doesn't result in any savings—all this does is suspend the taxes you were supposed to pay for the first three to five years. After that, you must pay the value-added tax (VAT) due on everything you imported to conduct business.

In order to qualify for this dubious exemption, you have to make a list of all the materials you intend to import in order to do business: computers, cars, tables, etc., with as thorough a description as possible, including the cost. If you import something slightly different or at a different price, you might have issues importing it.

Obviously, gathering this information is timely, cumbersome, and expensive. Perhaps worse, it removes the flexibility and the freedom required to act swiftly, which is an absolute necessity when starting a business. Instead you're stuck waiting for the approval of some official—unless you want to pay full taxes right away at customs, of course.

And by the way, if your business fails? Tough. Pay up.

Nevertheless, people are excited about APIX and its promise. I can't think of a better way to illustrate just how bad conditions currently are.

The tax system in Senegal is exceptionally challenging. We're supposed to make fifty-three payments per year, which consumes an average of 416 hours per year to calculate and file—and takes 45 percent of profits from a small or medium-sized business. How many companies are likely to relocate operations from, say, Singapore or the Bahamas to invest in Senegal?

When we import raw material and packaging, we have to pay regular customs at the border. Standard tariffs are 45 percent on a copier and 28 percent to import a computer. My cost for basic business items is roughly 30–45 percent more per item than what I pay in the United States. After investing considerable time and money, I did eventually find a well-meaning customs official who found a one-year exemption on imports for new businesses, but with the following conditions:

The exemption only applies to materials being brought in to incorporate into your finished product, which must be exported as a finished product within one year.

The company must have a validated industrial manufacturing and warehousing site (something startups rarely have).

Ninety percent of your annual production needs to go to exportation, with 10 percent going to the local market. This applies even if there is no viable local market for that 10 percent. If you want to export the remaining 10 percent, you have to solicit the approval of the general director of the customs office.

There needs to be a follow-up (a.k.a. government control) on repatriation of currencies (*suivi sur rapatriement des devises*), starting at three million CFA, which is roughly US$6,000. This is a step you need to take up with your bank. It's very cumbersome.

A government-licensed expert must determine your "manufacturing yield rate." That refers to the percentage of non-defective items of all produced items and is usually indicated by the ratio of the number of non-defective items against the number of manufactured items. In most manufacturing processes, you will end up with less than you planned for, with some losses due to, for example, spillage or evaporation. Perhaps a bad batch has to be discarded. By having a licensed expert (pre-)determine this percentage, the government is trying to avoid having you bring in more raw material than you need at the temporarily exempted rate. Complying with this requirement means we have to disclose our formulations and detailed production steps to third parties. These are our trade secrets, which we paid a lot of money to have developed during the research and development process. It is not hard to see why this would be very sensitive information to share with third parties, especially in environments where you can't always be sure of the integrity of those third parties. It is a risky proposition. So risky, in fact, that we decided as a company that the benefits of the savings we could get from choosing this route did not outweigh the risks.

◇◇◇◇◇◇◇◇◇◇◇◇◇◇

This decision was made somewhat easier by this simple fact: even if you wanted to hire one of these experts, you couldn't find one. Three years later I am still waiting for the high-ranking customs official to send me referrals for such experts or to give me pointers as to where to even begin looking for one. In his defense, I should point out that he is greatly embarrassed by the fact that he doesn't know where to find them, and further, no such source of information is indicated anywhere in the law. "You have to comply by using the services of a very specific X imposed by us, but we can't tell you where to find X. Good luck!"

If by some miracle you were able to find X, you would then approach the Minister of Industry to get an *admission temporaire exceptionnelle* ("exceptional temporary admission"), where they would require you to provide at least seven more documents.

A few things have probably changed since this happened a little more than three years ago, but you can see how heavy and senseless this process is. Moreover, try to imagine all the controls once you start, and the many times you have to file all types of records with various agencies, with most not available online. This is the "streamlined" version.

Meanwhile, for the part of my business that operates in the United States, I go online and get any supplies I want for my products almost instantly via Amazon, Home Depot, specialized suppliers such as Uline, or one of a thousand others, with no special permissions of any kind required.

Africa, like everywhere else in the world, needs leaders who say, "I'm going to make it easy for you to build new companies. I'm going to make it easy for you to hire and fire."

If you look at the Doing Business Index, you'll see that it is easier to do business in any Scandinavian country than it is anywhere in sub-Saharan Africa. That's why they're rich and we're poor.

Natural resources? We have mineral wealth and land wealth. We should be mind-blowingly rich, and we would be if we were unchained like those in Sweden.

You want to talk to me about "income inequality"? Here's my response: make the laws where I do business on an equal footing with those in wealthy countries. Take off the chains! Let us compete! Let us prosper!

Many nice people want to claim that education is the solution. But almost half of the ten million graduates churned out of the over 668 universities in Africa yearly do not get a job when they're done. That's according to Kelvin Balogun, the president of Coca-Cola–Central, East, and West Africa.[16]

If it is nearly impossible for entrepreneurs to create jobs, then it really doesn't matter how much we pour into education. The NGOs and governments can absorb only so many university graduates. Without an ecosystem that allows for the creation and growth of businesses, we have tens of millions of frustrated university graduates who are underemployed and poor. A university degree on its own, in the absence of a vibrant economy, does not feed the holder.

There is a saying in Senegal that the first job of a freshly minted university graduate is as a street vendor.

Okay, so if university degrees don't matter until we have a business environment that supports job creation, at least they can give us overly fertile Africans plenty of birth control so we don't keep having babies and overpopulate the planet, right? (Obvi-

---

16 "Unemployment in Africa: no jobs for 50% of graduates," African Center for Economic Transformation, April 1, 2016, https://acetforafrica.org/highlights/unemployment-in-africa-no-jobs-for-50-of-graduates/.

ously, this is not what I think—I have found that the "overpopulation" issue is the biggest worry that many Westerners have about Africa, on the rare occasions they actually think about Africa.)

Think again. First, many African women have lots of kids because they want to. Here is recent research by Dr. Melanie Channon:

> There is a strong tendency, in particular in the West, to assume that African women would have less children if only they had better access to contraception and high quality education and that rising population growth is caused by insufficient family planning. But this misconception presupposes that women want to have fewer children, which our research shows is often not the case.
>
> Increased access to contraception and education are important, but may not result in fertility declines as substantial as we have seen in other areas of the world.
>
> On average, nearly three quarters of women in African countries are failing to have the number of children that they want, but for many this is not down to a lack of contraception—they want more children not fewer. This is particularly common in Western and Middle African countries, where the average woman has over 5 children, but still wants more.
>
> Given the challenges that population growth in Africa present, we must listen to why women want so many children rather than just concentrating on providing family planning services. We need to recognise that access to contraception is not the "silver bullet" to tackling population growth that many believe.[17]

---

[17] University of Bath, "Access to contraception not 'silver bullet' to stem population growth in Africa," *ScienceDaily*, July 18, 2019, www.sciencedaily.com/releases/2019/07/190718145412.htm.

Why do African women want many children? Sometimes it's out of an abundance of maternal urge, but sometimes it's a good deal more pragmatic. For some women, these children (especially young children) are an insurance policy against divorce. All over the world, but especially in poor societies, women have turned to having children to keep their husbands. A husband is more likely to stay around, at least for a few more years, if he has another young child. There are greater social pressures not to abandon a mother with a young child. One of the main reasons a woman would want to keep her husband no matter what is the cachet it gives her in society but also the financial security it provides her, particularly in poor communities. That's why many women keep popping out babies.

There's more to it, of course. Poor women in poor countries have long chosen to have many children to provide insurance for their care and feeding when they're elderly. They have also long assumed, quite rightly, they would lose a few along the way. These days that's not as likely the case, but the behavior is still there.

If access to birth control is not a magic bullet for reducing birth rates, what will result in lower birth rates? Jobs for women—formal, paid jobs. I'll start with a jargony version from academia:

We find that the number of children below age six has a significantly negative effect on the woman's ability to work in the non-farm sector; it reduces the odds of employment of African mothers by 6 percent. The effects of the number of young children on women's non-farm work are more prob-lematic for older women and for women with more years of education. These findings imply that investments in family planning are likely to enhance the opportunities for women to work for pay and that policies aimed at facilitating the combination of child rearing and paid labor are particularly important for educated and older women.[18]

Imagine that! Having many young children makes it tough to work a job! Birth control has a bigger impact when women have opportunities to work for pay. Do you want to reduce the population boom in Africa? Help us get access to economic freedom so we entrepreneurs can create more jobs already!

It doesn't matter if you have six kids or none if there are no jobs!

And don't even get me started on the massive youth unemployment problem we have in Africa.

Jobs—jobs!—remain the best way for women to raise themselves out of poverty. Jobs allow women to have the financial independence they need so they are no longer dependent on men. Once we no longer need men for financial support, many of us can afford to take our time before getting pregnant and marrying. Even if we are already married, we can avoid getting pregnant because we do not need the man's income. Often husbands begin to support women working because they appreciate the increased household income as well. They also begin to consider the middle-class life that's possible if they invest more in the education of a few children rather than having many children.

Many believe that not having babies will allow girls to get a better education. But here's where I'm going to get politically incorrect again: the rise of billions out of poverty over the last thirty years hasn't been powered by education. It's the result of low-wage manufacturing (sometimes described as "sweatshops") and other factories. Don't like the notion? Fine. But understand

---

18 Eelke de Jong, Jeroen Smits, and Abiba Longwe, "Estimating the Causal Effect of Fertility on Women's Employment in Africa Using Twins," *World Development 90*, no. 1: February 2017: 360-368, https://doi.org/10.1016/j.worlddev.2016.10.012.

that's how the United States and Europe got rich too. Smoggy London during the Industrial Revolution provided the final dagger in the heart of feudalism. Nineteenth-century Massachusetts became wealthy because of its textile industry.

Do these initial factories provide good pay and working conditions? By today's Western standards, no. But they're a first step because, you know, *life is hard*. It's harder for the poor. And it's hardest of all when you don't have a job. The disdain for sweatshop jobs from Westerners who enjoy good, cushy lives has not helped the global poor. It is as if the person living in a mansion today claims that now everyone has to live in a mansion, too, because, you know, it is so much nicer! Everyone should have a pool, a home cinema, a home gym, etc. Yes, it would be nice if everyone who wanted such things could get access to them. But unless you were born with a silver spoon in your mouth, most of us will start adult life with a roommate and then move into a tiny apartment of our own, followed by possibly buying our first small home, and so on and so forth. That's how you eventually get to your mansion.

The low-wage factory job is just the first step, but it's an oh-so-crucial first step. Most people who are free of sweatshops come from families where their parents, grandparents, and great-grandparents worked in sweatshops, proudly raising each following generation to better conditions. Unless the work site is unhealthy or dangerous, there is no stupid job. It is immoral to deny poor people their first step to a better life.

Finally, consider how important job creation is for wildlife. Consider the chimpanzee population, for example. They will likely be extinct in a few decades because of loss of habitat (poor people gathering firewood) and people's desire (and need) for bush meat. When rural Tanzanians are hungry, they hunt chimpanzees and cook them on a fire built by cutting down the habitat. But if you give them a job in an urban environment, the problem goes away.

People who care about sustainability should be begging for more open markets in Africa. If you want more trees planted in Africa, help me make sure African women have normal jobs so they can buy modern stoves for their homes. That way they won't have to hack down trees to make charcoal to cook over to feed the household.

And just in case you happen to be one of those people who cares as much (or more?) about African human beings as you do about African wildlife, here's something you need to know: modern stoves save lives. Have you ever been inside a small home in which a woman is cooking food using charcoal?

It is a cancer factory.

I see propane stoves as one of the greatest public health gifts we can provide for hundreds of millions of African women. Sure, electric stoves powered by solar with enough battery backup to be reliable would result in fewer carbon emissions—but come back to me in ten, twenty, or thirty years when this is actually possible for hundreds of millions of people across the continent. In the meantime, access to clean-burning propane is growing rapidly—or would be, if the West wouldn't choke off the supply.

So sometimes I wonder, *Is everything lost?*

Why isn't the need for economic freedom in Africa a mainstream cause, supported by 100 percent of the people? No one—and I mean *no one*, left or right—would support the imposition here in the United States of the senseless laws that prevent economic development in most African countries.

Any serious human rights activist should also be an activist for greater economic freedom in Africa. Any serious environmental rights activist should also be an activist for greater economic freedom. But where are the activist crowds who are passionate about economic freedom? Anyone who is sane ought to care about improving the African business environment.

We just need to get people to listen.

CHAPTER ELEVEN

Ay du yem ci boppub boroom. (A conflict is not confined to the one from whom it originates.)

◇◇◇◇◇◇◇◇◇◇◇◇◇◇

N 2016, I HAD ANOTHER LIFE-CHANGING MOMENT. This was soon after Arianna Huffington's company abandoned me, leaving me with piles of useless products. My spirit was really, really down. I kept asking myself, *What do I do? Where do I go with this?* In truth, I didn't have the energy to go forward.

I was also depressed because a number of Black men had recently been killed by the police. Alton Sterling, a father of five, was gunned down in Baton Rouge. The next day, Philando Castile was shot. Castile was the 136th Black person who had been killed by the cops that year.[19] And there were videos. You had to watch, and then you had to rage.

I became obsessed with what could be done to stop it. More people would open their eyes to the issue following the death of George Floyd in 2020, but even before that there was a significant subset of us determined to do something about it.

---

19 Jon Swaine, et al., "Minnesota governor blames Philando Castile police killing on racial bias," *The Guardian*, July 7, 2016, https://www.theguardian.com/us-news/2016/jul/07/philando-castile-police-shooting-calls-justice-department-inquiry- fbi-minnesota-officers.

Michael and I took off for a weekend in the hill country outside of Austin, where Michael was going to participate in a closed session with John Mackey and a few others. They were hoping to figure out a way to move beyond political parties and partisan politics. It was all about reducing the growing political polarization. As Michael will tell you today, they clearly didn't have a great deal of success.

I wasn't invited, so I stayed in our hotel room. I spent hours consumed by Black Twitter, which was crazy agitated over the ongoing deaths and riots. I was listening to the people who were on the street participating because I trusted them more than the news.

It was bad. My Black friends were as anxious as I was. And then a friend of mine, someone I had always known as level-headed and open to everyone, spoke up. She posted a tweet saying we Blacks were fools to ever think "they" would regard us as equals. "It's never going to happen," she said. "From now on everyone has to choose sides."

There were many people saying the same thing, but I had known her to be so tolerant and level-headed. When I saw that from her and felt her pain, I was at the point of a breakdown. All I wanted to do was grab her and hug her. I was starting to go down the same path, believing we had to choose sides in the battle that was coming, believing that all was "Black" vs. "White" in a never-ending war.

So I was sitting there in the hotel, and the news came on that a Black man had just shot and killed five cops in Dallas. Another nine were wounded. It was a revenge shooting. The shooter said as much. The whole thing was crazy. But there it was. I found myself thinking, *Well, if they want war, they'll have war.* The moment I said that to myself, the door to our hotel room opened up, and who stood there? Michael.

Minnesotan, blond, blue-eyed Michael. My beloved.

I went into this hysterical laugh. Go to war with whom, exactly? With him and people who looked like him? Because of the skin they were born in?

That was when three thoughts spontaneously formed in my mind:

The first was: *Skin is skin.*

The next words were: *Go beyond.*

And then: *This is so ridiculous.*

It was at that moment that I snapped out of the darkness I was in. I had been headed for a dead and somber end. I still don't know what it would have meant for my marriage because I had sincerely thought, *Well, if I have to choose my camp, I have to choose my people!*

I said to Michael, "This is serious, and I'm going to do something about it. I can't accept that the only thing we can have is division."

And so, as with anything I'm serious about, I did the research. I went on a journey to discover why there is bias. I immediately discovered there is a thing called the science of bias—a study of how bias works. I started spending a lot of time poring through the works of a dozen or more brain scientists—behavioral scientists, psychiatrists, and especially evolutionary biologists and psychologists.

I learned that if you have a brain, you have biases. Biases begin very early in life and serve a very important function. Evolution tells us to best ensure your survival, you must first make sense of the world, especially by gaining the skills and knowledge to determine if a person or situation is a danger to you. The failure to do so means you may not be around the next second.

The role of the brain in this process is to help you do that as quickly and efficiently as possible, which it does through automation. For example, once the brain has figured out one plus one equals two, it will never waste the time to figure it out again.

By the time you're three years old, you're starting to categorize everything. That way you don't have to figure it out the next time. You only pause to deal with new situations; that's when your conscious mind kicks in. But for everything else, the brain assumes it knows the score. It makes most of your decisions for you, usually based on what it has already categorized. For example, it may have learned that "a Black man with a hoodie" may be dangerous. You're not even conscious your brain is doing this, but you cross the street to avoid the Black man anyway. Yes, you have biases. So do I. After all, our brains are data collection units intent on ensuring our health and happiness.

The news you watch and read is constructed to take advantage of this predisposition, which is why "if it bleeds, it leads." It's also why the producers choose a mugshot for the Black kid who was caught ripping off bread from the grocery store and the high school graduation picture of the White kid who just murdered his young family and dissolved them in acid. The former is a criminal. The latter is sick. Horrifically unjust, to be sure. The brain, with its natural mechanisms hardwired since birth, is the hardware. The software it runs on is your cultural imprint, which is everything that goes into the brain from your environment, including visual and verbal information and every experience since the day you were born.

You may have seen the video of the psychological study in which young Black girls are given two Barbie dolls. With the exception of their skin tone—one is white, the other brown—the dolls are identical. The little girls are asked, "Which is pretty? Which is nice?" Over and over they choose the White doll. It is heartbreaking. They have been programmed, and the "real world" impact is this: if you're a White girl, it gives you confidence. If you're a Black girl, no confidence. But confidence is imperative. How do you do well on a school test without confidence? How do you handle relationships without confidence? How do you handle job interviews without confidence?

From there it's all downhill. Other people see this lack of confidence and the resulting failures and say, "See, they can't succeed." And they're right! It's a snowball.

If you're a cop, you may shoot a Black boy first and ask questions later. It is brutally unjust—and it is often unconscious.

But that same cop may not have the same information encoded in his brain about a White boy. The hard drive in his head provides a message that the boy probably just needs help, or maybe he has a mental illness. Help him! Again, this is brutally unjust—and again, it is often unconscious. So he doesn't shoot the White boy.

Unconscious bias is basically a habit. The neurons have created a pathway—a shortcut—and in that pathway lives the habit. But it's not just a habit. It's a bad habit—an evil habit.

So how do you get rid of a bad habit? First, you have to acknowledge that you have this habit. Second, you have to decide you don't want it. But when you live in today's society, acknowledging you have a bias is dangerous. If you admit you don't trust a woman wearing a hijab, right away you might lose your job. Or be ostracized. But nevertheless, you have the ability to deal with the habit. Think of it as determination combined with reminders.

In order to remove your biases, you have to be mindful. You have to switch your conscious brain on; otherwise it remains in autopilot where all the biases live. You have to be reminded to stop the brain in its tracks.

Stop. Think.

It's an effort.

I found it helpful to understand the foundations of bias in evolutionary psychology. It didn't reduce the injustice. But it provided me with an explanation of what was going on—and the first inklings of a strategy for reducing this bias.

Once I understood this, I was like, *Oh my god*. But at least we are all in it together. We're not inherently bad. We just need to pay attention.

Like so many things brought about by evolution, including our ravenous desire for sugar and fat, these biases are declining in survival value. In today's world we don't need fight or flight. (How many bears have you run into lately?) We have to transcend that instinct.

And you can transcend it, especially if you know how it works. It is possible to undo a lifetime of cultural coding. As with any bad habit you want to transcend, you have to be able to say, "Okay, I have this bad habit—in this case, biases." Then you need to create reminders to switch off the autopilot in your brain. From there, you can follow a sort of mindfulness practice made of five exercises, scientifically designed to rewire your brain to free yourself of stereotypes. The process to rewire the brain takes approximately one year. The whole thing is beyond fascinating.

To understand this issue and be able to use its associated solution, we have to create a culture in which it is all right to recognize our biology. We have to be able to admit, "I've got a brain; therefore, I've got biases," without being accused of all types of "isms." The cancel culture we are deep in does not make this critical step easy. That's why I decided to build a brand rather than an NGO or other organization of that kind. Brands have such power to affect culture. In this case, if I could make it culturally acceptable to say, for example, "I've got biases," that would be a beautiful thing.

So I set out to create a new brand. I wanted to build something cool. And that's how my new company, SkinIsSkin, came to be.

I chose a lip balm as our flagship product because it's so well suited to what I have in mind. It serves as a little Jiminy Cricket in your pocket. A portable conscience. The message is, "Skin is skin." No messing around.

Every time you pull it out, you remember, and you think about your biases. People who know the story behind SkinIsSkin and who use it tell me they are reminded to be careful with their thoughts. Sometimes that mindfulness lasts five minutes. Sometimes two seconds. The most important thing is regular reminders, however brief.

There were other reasons for choosing a lip balm. First, I wanted to stay in skin care where I had established connections. Second, the product needed to be small so users would carry it with them everywhere. Third, I also wanted a product for any gender, any age. You don't have to be a skin care freak. It's a simple product and something that's in everyone's life.

Lip balm to fight discrimination!

That work is continued in the product naming style: "Mint and Curiosity," "Anise and Empathy," "Coconut and Love." Why? Because brain studies show the most effective way to disrupt a neuronal pathway—to break a bad habit—is to serve up these thoughts with love, curiosity, and empathy. When you call up these feelings, very different parts of your brain light up. It is profoundly different to look upon someone with curiosity rather than with fear. The first opens you up; the latter closes you down.

So as a brand and through our messaging, we make it okay to say, "Yes, I've got biases, and I'm going to rewire my brain to fix them."

And now you've also got a little cricket in your pocket as a companion on the journey.

◇◇◇◇◇◇◇◇◇◇◇◇◇

The relationship of Black Africans and African Americans is difficult. For the most part, Black Americans don't think about

Black Africans. Not consciously, at least. But I've always believed the view of others in the United States and in Europe regarding Blacks is highly influenced by how they view Black Africa. They see poverty and disease as inherent in Black populations; that spills over into their view of all Blacks everywhere. The alt-right takes advantage of this, saying you can't point out a Black self-governed entity that is fully developed. According to them (and echoing Trump), Africa is full of "shithole countries."

If there was one single reason for Blacks in the West to care about Africa, this would be it. We should share the goal of seeing African Blacks and Western Blacks financially succeed. It's imperative. It's a hard truth, but a truth nonetheless: money equals respect. Money equals power. Money equals freedom.

In July 2020, the Smithsonian Institution posted on its website a graphic called "Aspects and Assumptions of Whiteness." This graphic, a kind of digital poster, declared that hard work and rationality are characteristics of White people, which leads naturally to the obvious and obnoxious conclusion that these skills and principles are not so present in Black people.

An uproar quickly arose, and the graphic was pulled down. I watched the drama closely because I was so furious at the Smithsonian. I found it curious, but not unusual, that the most vocal critics were American conservatives, while liberals were largely silent.

I also want to point out—and this is much more distressing—that the only people I saw complaining were White. I posted the Smithsonian's image on my Facebook page, where I expected many of my 250 Black friends would express their outrage. Only one commented.

I called Ibou in Senegal. I told him the source of the poster and explained why it was a big deal. I said, "I'm just going to read it to you, from top to bottom. Without comment. Just listen."

So I read it to him: "To be White is to be logical. To be White is to believe in hard work. To be White is to be rational."

When I was done, he just said, "Then I guess I'm White."

He went on to say the people who wrote it are inhuman because these are the things that it takes to be a well-rounded human being. These are the character traits that everyone needs to succeed in life and to lead a good, honorable life.

Then he concluded, "I don't know what to tell you other than to say that my heart is hurting. This is terrible, and this is wrong."

Ibou wasn't an ascetic but rather was a man with few wants and needs. Me? I desperately wanted someone held accountable for that Smithsonian post.

Often Black Americans ask, "Why didn't I get one of the good jobs?" Yes, racism plays a role, but here is another part of the answer: because the Smithsonian has been out there telling corporate bigwigs that you're going to be a terrible employee. That it's not possible for you to be on time, not possible for you to think rationally. Who would put people like that in a responsible position? No one.

After I posted my comments about the Smithsonian graphic, a Black African immigrant friend called me. He's a respected man on the continent, with a significant role in Western media covering Africa. He called to tell me he has always stayed voluntarily out of African American questions altogether because to him all we share is skin color. Other than that, we are completely different. He isn't the only one who believes that. That's how many Black Africans feel about African Americans. I was raised to believe that African Americans have no culture and no learning. That they are violent people—"thugs" is the word often used. Up to no good. Negative stereotypes about African Americans are alive and well in Black Africa. Bias by Blacks toward Blacks very much exists.

I've lived in Europe and the States long enough to have engaged with American Blacks and to have gotten to know many intimately. And as with any other group of people I have been blessed to know, many are great, and some are not.

But if we really want to reduce bias toward people with black skin, those of us with black skin need to succeed at higher rates. No amount of Ibram Kendi-style anti-racism propaganda will change that. Remi Adekoya, a Polish Nigerian writer, notes:

> Whether it is Libyans selling black Africans into slavery, which is happening *right* now, Chinese people contemptuously discriminating against blacks in China, or Indians doing [the] same in India, a general low regard for black people across the world does seem to be a constant. In fact, the reason we focus on racism in the West and not elsewhere is because western societies are the most responsive to black opinion. As a general rule, the Chinese, Indians and Arabs don't seem to care very much whether we consider them racist or not. Their societies are openly assertive of their felt superiority.[20]

He goes on to note that only when Black Africa becomes prosperous will Black people begin to be respected around the world.

Yes, false stereotypes exist. I've created a company based on reducing biased perceptions. But no amount of "fighting bias" can overcome the everyday perceptions that people have. Decades ago there were many negative stereotypes concerning Chinese and Indian immigrants. A century ago there were common negative stereotypes concerning Jewish, Irish, Italian, and Eastern European immigrants (remember Polish jokes?). The negative stereotypes still exist here and there, but not like before. Now there are stereotypes of Indian Americans as Silicon Valley entrepreneurs and CEOs. Is anyone below the age of forty even aware of the

20 Remi Adekoya, "Has BLM picked the wrong target?" UnHerd, June 29, 2020, https://unherd.com/2020/06/why-dont-black-lives-matter.

stereotype of Indians as ragged, begging gurus with long beards, skinny legs, and long fingernails? Not when the CEOs of IBM, Google, Microsoft, Adobe, MasterCard, Nokia, PepsiCo, Deutsche Bank, etc., are Indian.

It doesn't come with lowering standards to ensure "equal participation." Lowering standards only means that when I work hard and smart, it won't matter because everyone around me is going to think I was given a handout. As economist Glenn Loury notes:

> I'm an economist. I've been teaching at Ivy League institutions for the last quarter century, and I'm pretty good at what I do. My papers appear in the top journals. Some of them have been cited thousands of times. I wouldn't mind winning the Nobel Prize in economics one day but it's very unlikely to happen. No African American has ever won the Nobel Prize in economics. Suppose Black Lives Matter were to go to Stockholm and picket the committee that decides who gets the Nobel Prize. The honor that I would like to be able to bask in would become unattainable were there even a *hint* of political influence.[21]

◇◇◇◇◇◇◇◇◇◇◇◇◇◇

I understand the people who advocate for affirmative action; they worry about equal access to opportunity for minorities. But I find this initiative to be too simplistic in its approach. I have never trusted or liked any outcome that relies on imposed quotas.

---

21 Michael Sandel and Glenn Loury, "The Question of Affirmative Action: An Interview with Glenn Loury," Quillette, December 16, 2020, https://quillette.com/2020/12/16/the-question-of-affirmative-action-an-interview-with-glenn-loury.

In the case of affirmative action, the Black person who got in simply to meet a quota will surely lag behind and will feel horrible as a result. It's demonstrably the case that Blacks do worse on the whole at Ivy League schools, with higher dropout rates.

How did affirmative action help this person? Instead, the same person could have been thriving if put into an environment that was a better match, unencumbered with a quota. If what you care about is seeing this Black person thrive in life, then it wouldn't matter that this person goes to Harvard but rather that this person goes to the best place and environment for them—the place where they have the maximum chance to thrive. Many people have not gone to Harvard and are doing just fine, thank you very much—sometimes better than those who went. Many entrepreneurs, including Mark Zuckerberg of Facebook, John Mackey of Whole Foods Market, Bill Gates of Microsoft, Richard Branson of Virgin, and Steve Jobs of Apple, dropped out of college.

Or consider the case of the Black person who made it into Harvard without affirmative action. They have to sustain the suspicion of others, including well-meaning people, that they may be at Harvard thanks to the quota—as a token, not because they earned it. This is degrading and so unfair.

Some who advocate for affirmative action may say, "This very deserving Black person might never have made it to Harvard because their merit would have been trampled by racism." But I am one who believes that a first step to success is to "be so dazzling they can't ignore you."

I can see how affirmative action might have been a first step at one time. It was the only way to work around the profound racism of some of those in the position of power to decide admissions. But today, it is time to transcend it for a fairer system for all. We should first ask ourselves: do we seek to ensure the individual thrives? If so, we need to understand that we need to undertake a complex case-by-case approach specific to each human being. If the system has the odor of politics, it is almost certainly ill considered.

That's why I advocate for school choice. I want to see each child offered so many educational choices they can choose one almost custom-made for them—one suited to their special genius and their dreams and goals in life. The goal should be to give every child, of any skin color, the equal opportunity to develop in the way that suits them best. There are 7.8 billion geniuses in this world, each different from the others.

I agree with virtually everything Thomas Sowell and Glenn Loury have to say regarding the path for Black success. Their basic message is, "Pick yourself up, dammit, by the bootstraps."

That's great, but they don't always give Black people concrete ways to do so. They don't even want to acknowledge one very plain fact: yes, there is racism in the West, and it sucks, and it does make life harder.

But it's just one factor. Maybe they are afraid to acknowledge that it's a factor because they feel opening that door would lead too many Blacks to walk through it on their way to victimhood.

What they need to say is, "Yes, there is racism, and yes, it causes pain. I get it. I hear you." That would be a start. But more than that, they need to provide step-by-step concrete ways for Blacks to escape the poverty and the violence.

I think one of the reasons I've been asked to speak at so many places and to visit with so many groups is because I speak the language of the intellectuals, but I bring the message to street level. I've lived the life of some of these people. I truly understand where they're coming from. I know some laws are terrible, and I know the impact they have.

Loury and Sowell and their fellow intellectuals don't always connect as well. They develop their research; they say, "The statistics find this; the facts say that," but to the kids in the streets of Baton Rouge or on the south side of Dallas, it all means nothing.

Yes, Thomas Sowell was born into poverty, but he wasn't born into the same type of poverty and culture these kids find themselves in.

Let's say you were born to parents who were both drug dealers in New Orleans. When you were five, your dad committed suicide, and your mom started using the drugs she was selling. Now she spends every day sick on her couch. By this point you're nine years old, and you have to feed yourself and your little brother. You're in constant survival mode. That all has consequences.

Some conservatives seem to be telling the young people, "No matter what has happened to you, you are responsible now for what you do," but provide no other tangible, concrete steps as to how to *be* responsible.

◇◇◇◇◇◇◇◇◇◇◇◇◇◇◇◇

So the kids naturally respond, "But what do I do? Where do I go?"

I prefer the words of someone like Bishop Omar Jahwar, my recently deceased friend, who always said, "No matter what happened to you, you're responsible for what you do for you." But he didn't stop there. His team today continues his work, helping young people turn their lives around by personally mentoring them.

The Bishop Omars of the world not only reassure the kids with, "I will support you in doing the right thing," but they actually roll up their sleeves to get in there with the kids as they work to pull themselves up. I feel like that's the part that's missing.

We have to understand there are things that are missing from their lives, things that—if we truly want to help—we have to provide. Imagine growing up in a household where the threat of being randomly shot at any point is real. Imagine children so deprived of parental guidance they enroll in first grade unable to name a single color.

But the worst of all are the people who say to these kids, "We're so sorry about what happened to you. There is nothing wrong with you. If you don't have a great job, it isn't your fault. All the bad choices you have made and continue to make are not your fault. It's all because of racism—and racism alone. Remain the way you are, bad choices and all. There's nothing you can do about it."

The person who says, "You don't need to change—the system does," is not a friend of the person they are speaking to, no matter their skin color.

Can you imagine anything more destructive than getting a kid to believe that nothing can change their situation no matter how hard they try? It is even more destructive for Black kids. This is regarded as "compassionate," but it is not ultimately compassionate.

If today everybody walking around us was not racist anymore—if you took a magic wand and waved it and suddenly everyone transcended racism—the shootings on the south side of Chicago would still happen. Those kids would still be dead.

One camp tells the kids to sit around (or should I say, continue on their destructive path) while they wait for the circumstances around them to change. The other camp tells the kids to just pick themselves up by the bootstrap, not accounting for any particular circumstances. Both camps are problematic and do not help much with this issue. The first creates a toxic dependency, and the second inspires resentment. Both sides need to integrate.

We need a voice—a loud voice—saying, "I totally empathize with what you're dealing with. I know where you came from. That being said, you don't have to be burned by the fire. There are ways to escape, and I will support you. But you—you!—will have to do the hard work."

That's the message we need to deliver. One of the reasons I respect Bishop Omar and his team is that they get up close and personal with kids being drawn into the gangs and give them real love, attention, and mentorship—*and* tell them that they are responsible for their actions! They provide the best of both worlds, and it results in dramatic reductions in gang violence.

The constellation of negative stereotypes attached to black skin is closely linked to the constellation of negative stereotypes attached to Africa. Simply put, often when one sees a Black person, he also consciously or subconsciously sees famine, wars, violence, and destitution.

In the end, I blame the poverty in the majority of African countries for this poor image the world has of us. Just forty years ago, China was poorer than most African nations today. China was held in utter disrespect. You may (and should) despise the Chinese Communist Party, but no one believes the Chinese aren't smart, hard-working people.

That's what becoming an economic powerhouse does; it's the same with so many other nations around the world. Ireland was a joke. Now it's wealthy.

In 2020, I posted an article on Facebook that points out that the 1.3 billion Africans together generate a gross domestic product that is less than the GDP of Britain, which has 66 million people.[22] If you want to know where racism comes from, look at those statistics. If you see people who are destitute, have less education, and have a very distinct skin color, your perception can very easily manifest as racism. It's the typical disdain for the poor. If that sounds harsh, look at the example in reverse: consider the absurd respect people show to the wealthy.

A hundred years ago the Chinese were treated almost as badly as we were. But since then, the Chinese have become rich and

---

22 Remi Adekoya, "Has BLM picked the wrong target?" UnHerd, June 29, 2020, https://unherd.com/2020/06/why-dont- black-lives-matter/.

prosperous. Hell, Hollywood won't even make a movie they think the Chinese won't like. They're deciding what we and the rest of the world can see and do.

Why? Because they have the money!

Ninety percent of the Black people in the world live in sub-Saharan Africa, which is one of the poorest places on earth. Skin color naturally gets connected with poverty; people assume Africans are inferior.

Nana Akufo-Addo, current president of Ghana, said it very well: "The destiny of Black people, wherever they are in the world, is linked to Africa. As long as Africa is not respected, Black people will not be respected."

If you really care about racism and the way Black people anywhere around the world are viewed, help me make Africa rich.

In an ideal world, we would love and respect our fellow human beings based on the content of their character, free from any concerns about the size of their bank accounts. That's a great goal to work toward. But first things first.

WITH BISHOP OMAR

CHAPTER TWELVE

Dund gu jeexagul, lu nekk xaj na ca. (While life has
not yet finished, all is still possible.)

◇◇◇◇◇◇◇◇◇◇◇◇◇◇

O
F COURSE, IN THE END the revivification of Africa
will be in the hands of Africans.
There is some good news: a recent survey found 76
percent of 4,200 young Africans want to start a business within
the next five years. Six in ten already have an idea percolating
for either a business or a social enterprise! Ivor Ichikowitz, who
manages the family foundation that conducted the survey, called
the results "a wakeup call for skeptics." Here's what he had to
say in an interview with CTGN America:

> There are many people who still talk of Africa as the
> Dark Continent; there are still many who talk of Africa as a
> hopeless case. The images of Africa are of starving children.
> Nobody sees optimism, but we've always seen it exactly the
> opposite way.
>
> I wanted to put some science behind this instinct that we
> had that this continent is going through this transformation
> and that there really is hope [and] optimism for a bright future
> for this continent. We took a huge risk in doing the survey

because we didn't know what the results would be, and we've been extremely vindicated. I'm excited to say that we really have found a continent that is truly filled with confidence and hope, especially this generation. This is the first generation of Africans eighteen to twenty-four years old who have never experienced colonialism, who have never experienced apartheid, who have never experienced extreme oppression, and this comes out in their hopes and aspirations, and in the positive energy we're getting out of the results of the survey...

[Young Africans] are in a space where they're connected to the world. There's a sense of connectedness to the global society, to the global economy, that I don't think has ever been seen before on the continent. There's also a sense of self-capability. In the past there's been a tendency for Africans to wait for others to come and solve their problems. We're seeing the exact opposite today. This is a generation who believes they have their future in their own hands; that they have the power and the capability to create their tomorrow as they want to see it.

It's also a generation that believes in democracy. It's a generation that believes they should have a say, so they believe in the principles of democracy—but not necessarily as the West sees it. It's almost split down the middle. Half the population wants to see a Western-style democracy while the other half of the population wants to see stable, autocratic long-term leadership. So what it tells us is, this is a generation that wants an African-style democracy, not necessarily a Western style of democracy.[23]

---

23 "Ivor Ichikowitz talks about African youth survey," Feb 26, 2020, CGTN America, https://www.youtube.com/watch?v=fYRJpVJzCjg&ab_channel=CGT-NAmerica.

That's a good description of the Cheetah Generation that George first spotted and named.

I also want to give a shoutout to the extraordinary initiatives of young tech Cheetahs who are springing up around the continent, especially in Anglophone nations (we Francophone nations are definitely lagging behind). Nigeria, Kenya, Ghana, and South Africa have developed vibrant tech ecosystems. Kenya launched M-Pesa in 2005, one of the first mobile-based money systems. By 2010, it was the most successful one in the developing world. In 2013, Hopstop, founded by a Nigerian tech entrepreneur, was sold to Apple for $1 billion. Calendly and City Block are also both Nigerian-owned unicorns (startup companies), each with a valuation of a billion dollars or more (albeit not Africa-focused). More recently, in 2021, Flutterwave, a Nigerian fintech company, became the fourth African tech unicorn actually serving Africa— and the first one founded by a Black African—to achieve such a valuation while still a startup. In 2020, more than $1 billion was invested in African tech startups across the continent. The African tech scene is happening.

The first goal of our awareness-raising effort is to teach everyone—the West and my fellow Africans in particular—about the history of the African continent. As I've said, for many, it seems as if African history begins with the arrival of Europeans and later the Americans. But Africa was the home of great civilizations for thousands of years before that. I'm pleased that Henry Louis Gates, a well-known Harvard professor, recently produced a six-hour documentary for PBS called *Africa's Great Civilizations*. (It's now available on Amazon Prime. And yes, this is a plug.) It provides a look at more than two hundred thousand years of African history and delivers it in an enjoyable, colorful way. That's invaluable given most of the other available resources are academic and are therefore often boring, if not off-putting.

Gates does it notably well, particularly for our purposes. He points out, for example, that all human beings descend from African roots. All eight billion of us are cousins! Gates also points out that Africa is the source of much of what makes us human, including writing and art and music. The early Egyptian kingdoms were decidedly Black African, including the pyramid builders. Amanirenas, the queen of the African kingdom of Kush, defeated the great Roman army of Augustus Caesar in a withering five-year war lasting from 27 to 22 BCE.

Mansa Musa, the fourteenth-century emperor of Mali, was the richest man in the world—and likely of all time! It was largely through trade in gold and salt that Mansa Musa gained his wealth, which he used to conquer new lands but also to create in Timbuktu not just a great trading center but also a city of universities and scholars. Mansa became famous throughout the world for his prominent inclusion in the *Catalan Atlas*, published in 1375 and still regarded as the most important map of the ancient world. Regarding his wealth, it is said that while making his *hajj* (pilgrimage) to Mecca, he gave away sufficient gold in Cairo to deflate the value of gold across Asia and Africa.

The first university in the world was founded in Fez in 859 CE, predating Oxford by at least one hundred years. The University of Sankore in Timbuktu, now in present-day Mali, evolved from a mosque founded in 989 CE. Under Mansa Musa, it developed one of the largest libraries in the world—certainly the largest in Africa since the Library of Alexandria.

As Gates says, these and other magnificent accomplishments provide a "profound refutation" to the belief that Africa had no history before Europeans arrived: "This continent has always been a dynamic, interconnected and integral part of world history."

This interconnectedness was built and maintained as it always is: through trade and commerce. African civilizations grew great on the east coast through trade with Asia. Between 800 and 1600 CE, an estimated five hundred tons of gold, much of it collected from the continent's interior, moved through eastern ports. The west coast tied itself to Europe and the Americas.

Of course a mere six hours (the length of the series) must by necessity give short shrift to the full history of African civilizations and to the trading centers and trading routes that once made Africa a world center of commerce. When giving my talks and in my other writing I often turn to the work of Ibrahim Anoba, the editor at Africanliberty.com and an important guide into the world of African philosophy and history. Here is a quick history of a few of Africa's most important centers of power, which I'm including as what I readily acknowledge is a far-too-brief introduction to Africa's precolonial history.

[Kush] flourished between 785 BCE until its declination in 350 CE and it was one of the most prosperous early African civilizations. Kush has a special place in Black history. It was one of the earliest—if not *the* earliest—Black civilizations with complex economic and political processes. It rose to prominence and maintained relevance throughout the ancient world with its exploits in trade and commerce until its destruction by the Kingdom of Aksum—another early African civilization with a fascinating history of trade and religion...[24]

At one time Aksum, located on the east coast of the Sudan, was "unparalleled" by any other African kingdom except Egypt.

At its height, though, the Aksumite Empire pioneered remarkable innovations in commerce, and its influence was so far-reaching that historians believe its territory extended

---

24 Ibrahim Anoba, "Commerce and Trade in Ancient Africa," https://www.libertarianism.org/columns/commerce-trade-ancient-africa-egypt.

beyond the boundaries of contemporary Ethiopia, Sudan, and Eritrea. Later, around the sixth century CE, the Aksumite territory spread into Southern Arabia and Yemen, although Aksum's presence in Arabia would be cut short by a Persian invasion of southern Arabia. Its strong navy protected the coastal trade routes and the trade networks along the Nile River and the Southern Red Sea, which were the source of its tremendous wealth. The strength of Aksum was well captured in the account of the influential Persian prophet of the third century CE, Mani, where he wrote: "There are four great kingdoms on earth: the first is the Kingdom of Babylon and Persia; the second is the Kingdom of Rome; the third is the Kingdom of the Aksumites; the fourth is the kingdom of the Chinese."[25]

I want to add two more: Because of its location and ready ports, Kilwa, an island located in modern-day Tanzania, dominated the trade that swelled the treasuries of those along the Swahili Coast. It was the African port of arrival for goods from Arabia, Persia, and India. In turn it was the port of departure for the gold that was coming from the kingdom of Great Zimbabwe. Trade made Kilwa a center of eastern commerce from the fourteenth century to the sixteenth century, when the Portuguese arrived.

Great Zimbabwe was also a flourishing kingdom, with its heyday ranging from the eleventh to the fifteenth centuries. Its name, Zimbabwe, is a Bantu word for "stone houses," a reflection of the city's vast stone constructions, whose great size and astonishing craftsmanship convinced the earliest Western visitors to the site that the local tribesmen could not

---

25 Ibrahim Anoba, "Commerce and Trade in Ancient Africa: Aksum," https://www.libertarianism.org/columns/commerce-trade-ancient-africa-aksum.

have built them. These buildings were at the cutting edge of engineering and craftsmanship for their time. Archaeologists found objects from China and Persia at Great Zimbabwe, indicative of truly astounding trade routes.

The moral of this story: trade, trade, trade allowed our earlier empires to become prosperous. And now African states all have high tariff barriers? What is wrong with this picture? The African Free Trade Agreement, which has been signed by most African nations in the past few years, will finally reduce the trade barriers (if actually implemented as promised by African leaders). But really, why did we need to wait for 2021 to get the free trade within Africa that was our birthright?

Worse yet, that agreement only addresses trade *within* Africa. Unlike the great past kingdoms of Africa, which traded globally, African nations will almost certainly continue to maintain high tariffs on goods from outside Africa.

As the ever-indispensable George Ayittey recently wrote on AfricanLiberty.org, economic freedom existed for centuries before the arrival of the colonists; indeed it was a fundamental way of life for virtually everyone in sub-Saharan Africa. The one primary distinction is that while "individual ownership was common," the African economic system often consisted of participating families, or as they are sometimes called, *the lineage.*

The means of production were owned by the lineage—a private entity separate from the tribal government—and thus privately owned. Land, for example, was lineage-controlled, giving rise to the myth of communal ownership, while hunting gear, spears, and fishing canoes were individually owned. Nevertheless, the extended family acted as a corporate unit, marshaled family labor, and decided what crops to cultivate on the family land. There was a sexual division of labor, and the cultivation of food crops was always a female occupation in traditional Africa, which explains why over 70 percent of Africa's peasant farmers today are women.[26]

Most of the trade was conducted in markets, which were of two classes. The local markets were mostly run by women, while the larger regional markets—the ones that connected the international trade routes—were mostly the province of men. Some of these regional markets grew into massive communities linking Africa with the world, including Timbuktu and Kano. As George wrote, these regional markets served the largest of the trans-Saharan caravans and grew vastly wealthy as a result. African goods included fabrics, pottery, and goods tooled from brass. And of course, there was the trade in metals, including "iron, gold, silver, copper, and tin." George describes the system as "Peasant Capitalism."

> The kente weavers of Ghana; the Yoruba sculptors; the gold-, silver-, and blacksmiths; as well as the various indigenous craftsmen, traders, and farmers were free-enterprisers. The natives have been so for centuries. The Masai, Somali, Fulani, and other pastoralists who herded cattle over long distances in search of water and pasture also were free-enterprisers. So were the African traders who traveled great distances to buy and sell commodities—a risk-taking economic venture.[27]

Peasant capitalism continued to operate in the peaceful pockets of colonized Africa for some time after the arrival of the Europeans and Americans. Many of these entrepreneurs were highly successful. In the end, too successful:

---

26 George B.N. Ayittey, "Indigenous African Free-Market Liberalism," https://www.africanliberty.org/2019/06/01/indigenous-african-free-market-liberalism.
27 George B.N. Ayittey, *Africa Unchained: The Blueprint for Africa's Future*, Springer, 2016, p. 350–51.

Not only were blacks better farmers but they were also competing with white farmers for land. Moreover, they were self-sufficient and hence not available to work on white farms or in industry, particularly in the Transvaal gold mines where their labor was badly needed. As a result a series of laws was passed that robbed blacks of almost all economic freedom. The purpose of these laws was to prevent blacks from competing with whites and to drive them into the workforce.[28]

The blood of individual liberty runs rich in the veins of African history. As we saw earlier, African tribes used a decentralized governance structure completely unlike the modern African state (which is essentially a European colonial import).

Yes, it's frustrating. People from all over the world travel to marvel at the Palace at Versailles. But when Louis XIV was at home, the place stank royally. Most of the aristocracy only took a bath once a year because they feared it would otherwise damage their skin. The aristocracy constantly tried to cover body odors with perfume, but you and I know that after a while, it only makes the odors worse. Their powdered wigs were full of lice underneath, and their stairways were piled with human excrement. But today we only talk about the furniture and the Hall of Mirrors.

When the people of the world talk about Africa, they only talk about the bad stuff. Imagine what the image of France would have been if all the stories had focused on elements such as the above.

Europe is beautiful; America is cool; Africa is a shithole.

---

28 Frances Kendall, Leon Louw, *After Apartheid: The Solution for South Africa*, 1987, quoted in Africa Unchained.

So I make it my job to focus on those parts of the story that have been forgotten. I want to show the world a beautiful place, with cities and villages as civilized as any in the world. Indeed, I want to show that Africans were often ahead of the times. I want to make it clear that if we had not been cut short due to slavery and colonialism, we might have continued to exceed the larger world. I don't mean some Wakandan fantasy, like in Marvel's *Black Panther* movie. I mean a place where the people are both flawed and good and where, maybe, we would have created world-changing ideas. Maybe we would have constructed a government that would have been superior to democracy as we know it today.

When the Europeans arrived in Somalia, they found a culture in many ways like their own. They found tribes that were collaborating. Did they fight sometimes? Of course. We are human. But for the most part, peace was maintained. There were royal courts, and kingdoms were expanded by strategic marriages. It was nothing like what we have today.

But when the European colonizers showed up, they said, "Oh, you bunch of savages, we're going to bring you civilization." So we went from a sophisticated decentralized system that prevented domination by strongmen to nation-states designed by colonizers. They introduced centralized systems of control, formal borders, and overarching laws that were and are prone to being corrupted.

The new colonial boundaries didn't match the tribal boundaries; instead, they were and are perfectly arbitrary. Whoever seizes power within the new borders gains power over the diamonds, oil, foreign aid, and everything else of value, including the other tribes. That's how democracy becomes a sectarian or ethnic battlefield.

Look at Rwanda. In the 1990s, some within the Hutu tribe (and others beyond the border) began agitating the Hutus. "If you are the majority," they said, "why do you have the Tutsi minority ruling over you?" You know what happened then. The Hutus murdered more than half a million Tutsis.

In the United States we mostly think of law as what the legislature passes. But for people who are serious about common law, including the British, the law is judge-made over centuries. Most African law was originally much more similar to a common law legal system. The newly imposed colonial "laws" were completely contrary to our traditions, which created unnatural pressures. That was when we moved from tribes to tribalism, the ongoing ethnic conflict of today.

That's where we stand now.

This is the history we need to teach about Africa: before the arrival of the colonists and slavers, Africa had a functioning free-market system connected to the major trade routes of Europe and Asia. The destruction of that system was intentional. It can be re-created now, and must be, for the sake of every generation of Africans.

Let me sum it up for you, dear reader. Call this my manifesto:

1. All prosperous nations must allow their people to create value through enterprise.

———

All nations protect property rights to ensure citizens and business owners are not in fear that criminals or the government will arbitrarily take their property. All nations allow their citizens to create business enterprises freely, without undue restrictions from government overseers. All nations allow their citizens and their enterprises to work within a stable legal framework, featuring relatively unbiased laws and courts that allow disputes to be handled fairly.

Most African nations do not provide these fundamental rights to enterprise. In international rankings of Economic Freedom and

Doing Business, only Mauritius, a tiny island nation that has now reached almost European levels of prosperity, is in the top tier. A few others, including Botswana and Rwanda, are moving in the right direction.

Most African nations are in the bottom half or even the bottom third (see page 191). Our nations are the worst in the world at providing economic freedom.

2. Africa should be filled with prosperous nations.

———

But why should it? Why should we care about Africa? Here is one reason, a very self-serving one for me—and for you, dear reader: a rising tide lifts all boats. If Africa is underproducing—and it is, grossly—the continent's citizens aren't the only ones who lose. It's often said in the United States that our greatest resource is our people. In a globalized world, the loss of the talents and energies of more than a billion human beings is incalculable. What could an unleashed Africa bring to every aspect of human endeavor? We have artists, philosophers, academics, businesspeople, and thinkers and doers of every kind just waiting to reveal their talents to the world! I believe there are eight billion geniuses in the world. Each of us came to this Earth with a unique genius, and that genius represents a part of the solution to humanity's problems. Any time a human being is deprived of manifesting their genius, all of humanity is diminished.

3. Africans must have a can-do mentality and work toward the goals of prosperity through a positive capitalist path forward.

———

We cannot succumb to a victimhood mentality. Both NGO forces and anti-capitalists can foster that victimhood mentality.

While some NGOs are focused on true empowerment, others too often approach Africans as pathetic objects in need of a White savior. They communicate this message both openly and indirectly.

Yes, it can be hard due to a lack of opportunity. Anti-capitalist intellectuals, both in Africa and abroad, endlessly repeat a victimhood narrative about Africa being poor due to slavery, colonialism, and ongoing exploitation. Yes, Africa has been victimized. But until and unless these same intellectual forces articulate and endorse the positive capitalist path forward—which will let us leave that past behind—they are part of the problem, not part of the solution. *They are the bad guys.*

◇◇◇◇◇◇◇◇◇◇◇◇◇◇◇

I wanted to manufacture products in Africa for two reasons: first, because I'm very interested in creating jobs back home, especially for high-end products that prove we can break the thatched-roof ceiling. I have to say that even for all of my boldness, it took me a while to get comfortable manufacturing in Africa.

It wasn't easy. I've often had to explain why we are doing it in Africa because most in the beauty industry have always seen Africa as a place for buying raw materials, not producing finished products. Yes, it drives me crazy sometimes. While I respect the traditions of indigenous African women, I cannot respect the West's fascination and fetishism for those of us who have not had the opportunity to move up the economic ladder. The best we can do for your delight is to collect shea nuts and then dance around the pots? You don't think we can do better than that?

We are doing better than that. Our workers have learned and put into practice world-class standards for producing quality products that can compete anywhere. That's how you get into Whole Foods and Nordstrom.

The products we make in Senegal have all the craft and elegance of hand-made and hand-poured, but with the rigor of a modern lab. Four years ago the women who now produce these fine products could never have imagined they would one day hold down jobs. Instead, they were waiting for husbands. Capitalism is the best thing that ever happened to feminism. Women can escape poverty—and bad husbands too.

I'm optimistic for my companies not just because the products are so good but also because the sales channel we built for SkinIsSkin is the same sales channel we'll use for Tiossan. So the groundwork is laid for Tiossan to come back. I don't know how, and I don't know when, but Tiossan happened in my life for a reason, and I need to remain true to it.

The second reason I wanted to manufacture products in Africa is admittedly more idealistic: if we don't shout about the need of the African people for dignity, who will? If you and I don't push for African prosperity, who will? Most African leaders are out to fill their own pockets. Most of those who are leading international aid organizations are unwilling to be full-throated advocates of African enterprise, independence, and self-respect. Even today the norm remains a condescending pity approach to Africans. We must be assertive and persistent leaders of this alternative movement.

I'm particularly hopeful we can get college students in America and elsewhere to participate, though I admit there is little evidence they will. They, too, are frequently caught up in the momentary enthusiasms—the preferred injustices of the day—and often cannot see beyond them.

But please: we're talking about lifting more than a billion Africans out of poverty. Who can't get enthused about that?

Let me return you once more to my factory and to the day I heard those awful words spoken by my young employee, Nafi: "My whole life I have always seen people like me represented in movies, magazines, and such as poor, hopeless people other people need to help. So I must confess that by now, I have come to believe that maybe us Black African people must be inferior."

But I also want to remind the reader why Nafi was able to tell me, "I am crying because now I know that it is not true. I am not inferior. Black Africans...we are not inferior." It is because each day she goes to a job where she is recognized as a valuable employee. She works in a spotless laboratory wearing spotless garments, including a gleaming white lab coat. She earns more money than she ever imagined possible doing a job she never believed she could one day have. She knows the products she makes are purchased by the coolest people in the coolest country in the world. And she knows they are willing to pay $8 for those little tubes—a decent day's wage in Senegal!—because she, Nafi, makes sure it's worth it.

As a Black African who routinely sees how we are disrespected around the world—and, yes, often regarded as inferior—the most important purpose of my life is to accelerate the small positive changes currently taking place in Africa so that in a few decades we can be respected as true equals, global co-creators of innovation and prosperity. The Chinese and the Indians are well on their way to achieving such status thanks in large part to pro-capitalist reforms they made in the 1980s and '90s. China has lifted itself from centuries of cursed poverty to serve as the only rival to the United States for world economic hegemony.

But other than some libertarian groups, I don't hear anyone calling for the liberation of Africa. I've described the benefits, but consider the drawbacks of doing nothing. China is even now extending its tentacles into Africa, often by buying off our politicians.

We in Africa have unlimited natural wealth, yet we are poor. A few years ago, Dubai was a pile of sand, and Hong Kong was a barren rock. Singapore was a swamp-filled jungle. How did some of the most worthless pieces of land become among the richest places on earth?

This book is my answer.

My most ardent hope is that we can finally agree that Africans deserve world-class business environments and world-class capitalist institutions, just like those enjoyed by the citizens of Denmark, New Zealand, Switzerland, and the United States. I beg of you, if you truly care about Black Africans, if you truly care about us, join me in being a forthright advocate for economic freedom in Africa.

As a consequence of our efforts, I see Africa launching manufacturing to rival Shenzhen, tech innovation to rival Silicon Valley, culture to rival New York and Paris, all with a *joie de vivre* that is uniquely African.

This is the Africa I live in—in my head and in my heart. The vision is clear, and the path to it is solid. We know how to make such a radical transformation, a transformation all of us will be able to witness in our lifetimes, because it takes only a few decades to take effect.

So let's finally free the Cheetahs, the fast runners of Africa. The only freedom we still need is economic freedom. And then let the world marvel as we Africans embark on the run of our lives, with leaps and bounds. It will be a most beautiful phenomenon to witness: an entire generation of Africans rising up to restore the lost prosperity and dignity of our beloved Motherland and the amazing culture our precolonial forefathers created.

I am Magatte Wade. I am a Cheetah.

And this is the content of my heart.

CHAPTER THIRTEEN

Pexe du jeex. (There is no end of solutions.)

◇◇◇◇◇◇◇◇◇◇◇◇◇◇

S O HOW CAN AFRICANS BECOME PROSPEROUS and known globally as co-creators of innovation and prosperity?

Here I'll outline my vision for the Cheetah Generation (fast-running African entrepreneurs and their allies). The goal of the Cheetah Generation is to call on all the Cheetahs of Africa, including those who have departed in search of greater freedom somewhere else (the Diaspora), to lead the transformation we seek for our people and land.

The Cheetah Generation will unite all the Cheetahs of Africa to work together, just as cheetahs do when they hunt. I love nothing more than watching a coalition of cheetahs hunting. You can only admire the level of patient, deep collaboration and superb coordination they showcase.

My only caveat is this: being a member of the Cheetah Generation has nothing to do with your age or whether you are African or not and everything to do with your mindset. We're going to move fast, like cheetahs. We're going to make progress in leaps and bounds.

The Cheetah Generation has two main arms. The first is building awareness, and the second is taking action.

BUILDING AWARENESS.

We need to organize and focus all who care about Africa to rally around pro-business, pro-growth strategies. We need to educate those who actually care about African people to engage in more constructive and less destructive (or merely pointless) activities. And we need to work with those who have been convinced that free markets are the key to African prosperity.

That's step one because too many people who want to help—like Jeffrey Sachs and the enthusiastic young people on college campuses—have no idea what's going on. They've all participated in efforts to provide a proper diagnosis and treatment regimen for Africa, but all their campaigns have been ineffective because they're treating the wrong disease!

This is true for Africans, too, because many Africans, particularly older Africans, have bought into the misguided understanding that the socialist independence leaders of Africa (Senghor, Nyerere, Nkrumah, etc.) and Western anti-capitalists have been promoting. Why shouldn't they? For decades everyone has been reading the same playbook—the same studies, the same theories. They see that the only ones who can survive in our overregulated systems are those who know someone in the government. Or you can make a nice living working with some of the NGOs, which are often part of the problem. Meanwhile, most of the African youth are frustrated and angry, especially at African leaders, with no solutions in sight other than to remove current leaders and put in place others (sometimes even putschists), who will probably perform just as poorly as their predecessors. This is a time bomb, and resentment toward leaders or the West won't get us anywhere unless we have a realistic positive direction.

CHOOSE YOUR POISON.

It's almost funny, really. Here are all these anti-business, anti-capitalist people who look at the poverty in Africa and say, "Look! Capitalism doesn't work." They still don't understand the difference between open markets (a.k.a. entrepreneurial capitalism) and crony business.

Have faith in the fact that as we make it easier to do business, a middle class will be formed. If we focus on liberating the entrepreneurs, they in turn will build this middle class by creating companies and jobs. And then the middle class can and will fight the last mile: greater individual rights, proper governance, all of that. That's the flow—that's the order in which things work.

It is a universal truth: if you're poor, people tend to treat you poorly, and it becomes harder to assert your normal human rights. It's not fair or right, but it is. They treat us poorly because we don't have much. But if you have a good middle class, all these battles will be fought by the middle class—the only entity that can fight this fight and win it. Why does it happen in the United States? Because there is a dominant middle class, with plenty of food in their bellies and roofs over their heads. They have money to invest in efforts toward change.

I'm currently head of the Center for African Prosperity of Atlas Network, the leading organization of African free-market think tanks. Atlas Network isn't a new organization; it's been around for forty years and has significant, stable funding. Many of the fifty-four nations of Africa (or fifty-six, depending on whether you count the two disputed nations, Somaliland and Western Sahara) have at least one free-market think tank, and they are all working to change the laws in their respective countries to remove barriers to entrepreneurship. It's incredibly important work. AtlasNetwork.Org is where you can go to learn more about issues related to economic freedom in Africa as laid out by our regional partners.

Regarding the effort to promote African entrepreneurship, I should also mention the African Diaspora Network, which is made up of African immigrants in the United States. They're mostly Silicon Valley entrepreneurs, which is good because they have resources. But it's limited because their efforts toward business development are naturally focused on digital solutions. Many of them don't always realize that the digital world has boomed in part because it is the least-regulated market in the world (which is why the internet took off). They remain mostly unfamiliar with the difficulties created by overregulation in Africa for all non-tech entrepreneurs who have way fewer possibilities to escape the regulations due to the simple fact that these tech entrepreneurs mostly operate in the cloud. But the Nigerian tech entrepreneurs are just now starting to feel how painful and stifling regulations can be with increased regulation of the tech sector in Nigeria (leave it to governments to try to kill the goose that lays the golden egg).

I gave a talk at one of their meetings, and as usual, I pointed out that the African regulatory system sucks. Thereafter, the meeting was a little awkward because they are encouraging others to invest in Africa, saying, "We're a great place to do business."

But I tell the whole story, including the all-important fact that the African business environment is lousy. A few people came up afterward to say, "Yeah, you're right," and shrugged their shoulders. But I don't see them changing their focus. And that's fine for them. There is money to be made in tech, but it quite simply doesn't have the same impact as manufacturing jobs, not least because it doesn't create the same number of jobs.

Tech alone is not going to create a fully prosperous Africa. I know we need other kinds of entrepreneurs evolving in environments that cannot yet escape their surrounding laws, which means we have to deal with the business climate. We need to be able to build houses and office buildings. We need the freedom to manufacture goods (this is what it means to build industries or industrialize), including the freedom to hire and fire freely. We need to be able to open businesses easily (and not just claim we have a twenty-four-hour one-stop shop to register a business, when in fact it takes months to gather the paperwork needed to take to the so-called one-stop shop). We need access to diverse kinds of financing structures (African states definitely overregulate banking and finance), and we need access to fair and timely adjudication for addressing business disputes.

So on one hand is an awareness-raising arm. The other arm is designed for taking action.

TAKING ACTION.

We will work with those who have been convinced that free markets are the key to African prosperity.

After I was featured in the movie *Poverty, Inc.,* I was approached by twenty to thirty organizations asking me to speak to them. They all had the same questions: what can we do? Buy African products? But where?

We missed out on a great opportunity by not having a working system in place to take advantage of this response. I don't want that to happen again.

So first we're going to provide a website (CheetahMade.com) where anyone can buy "Cheetah Made" verified products. These are African products, made in Africa by Africans, but we're also going to provide a great deal more. Recall that our priority isn't quick fixes but to change the system to allow for long-term prosperity for all. On our website, you'll be given concrete steps you can take to be part of the solution:

- Evangelize for the Cheetah Generation itself.
- Purchase "Cheetah Made" verified products.
- Invest in African companies.

- Mentor African entrepreneurs.
- Contribute talent or money to innovative ways to leapfrog education in Africa.
- Contribute talent or money to African e-government initiatives.
- Contribute talent or money to African Startup Cities initiatives.

It will come as no surprise that, after evangelizing for the Cheetah Generation, our first goal is ensuring that those throughout the world have an opportunity to quickly and simply purchase Cheetah Made products.

We already have a website set up for that—CheetahMade. com—and we will be adding items quickly. Those who want to participate will be able to buy some of the incredible products now produced by Africans—everything from premium skin care to beautiful jewelry to yummy teas to great swimsuits—even snacks we young African kids have always enjoyed but you never knew existed.

There are awesome peanuts that are roasted in hot sand in Senegal. Even the peanut butter from Senegal has a very special taste. Some women in Africa make incredible jams of hibiscus with strawberry and mint. And baobab jam! Baobabs are those huge, weird trees that seem to be upside down because their branches resemble roots. Baobab dried fruit is also great for making smoothies because it has powerful antioxidants. We also have coconut chips that are as addictive to munch on as potato chips—but much healthier! Everywhere you look in Africa you find cool stuff.

I'll stop now because I realize I sound like I'm making a pitch. And I am, I suppose. Let me just say this: the entire continent of Africa has long been completely ignored, and there is more happening there than you can possibly imagine.

We intend for Cheetah Made to support diverse African brands and companies.

Some of the other opportunities available through the Cheetah Generation will require a greater commitment: mentoring entrepreneurs in Africa, for example. We will be the go-between to help successful businesspeople around the world find and connect with entrepreneurs in Africa who are seeking mentorship and guidance for their businesses.

Those who are interested in investing in companies in Africa will be provided with guidance and connections on the ground. We are in contact with several credible funds that invest in African companies. See our website, CheetahGeneration.com, to get in contact if you are interested in learning more.

There will be no scams. There will be no White savior complex behavior. Just human beings who respect each other, engaging with one another at an eye-to-eye level, committed to the idea that win-win-win is the rising tide that lifts all boats. We want to do good, do well, and have fun together while we're at it.

And for you, my beloved African youth who are inspired by this vision, I have a special invitation for you to plug in however you please. We'll need African students, educators, entrepreneurs, mentors, funders, etc. In addition, e-government and Startup Cities will provide countless excellent jobs for ambitious, talented young Africans.

E-GOVERNMENT AND STARTUP CITIES.

Some of the opportunities available through the Cheetah Generation will obviously involve long-term projects.

Regarding e-governments, let me begin by pointing out that it is difficult to exaggerate how dysfunctional most African governments are. While many around the world are attached to a mythical notion of government as benevolent elected officials and efficient administrators laboring together in the public interest, this notion is laughable in many developing nations. In Africa, government jobs are often nothing more than a cushy sinecure, and political positions are often a license to steal.

What to do? One possible solution is e-government. From one perspective, e-government is simply a matter of making procedures more efficient, as technology has in every other industry. Why shouldn't the various bureaucratic agencies not be as efficient as Amazon or Google? Tiny Estonia, which just thirty years ago was a poster child for the backwaters of the world, is a global leader in e-government. TechReport estimates the nation now has 99 percent of all government services available online 24/7. Thirty percent of the population uses i-voting. Current estimates suggest that "the reduced bureaucracy has saved 800 years of working time."

Imagine if instead of waiting months to get approval from an African bureaucrat, an African entrepreneur could have instant access online? That would be a huge win.

But now imagine bigger: the ultimate e-government system would allow citizens to track all revenue and expenditures of their government. With a few exceptions, such as personnel decisions, every meeting would be recorded and every email made public. That means every procurement deliberation would be documented, and every receipt for every expenditure would be openly available. While such a system wouldn't eliminate graft, it would make it considerably easier to catch and identify the culprits. Politicians and bureaucrats would still steal, but over time the most egregious excesses could be eliminated.

Why would a politician ever allow such an encroachment on their gravy train? The best rationale would be leverage from the international donor community. Much of Africa remains heavily dependent on foreign aid. Instead of allowing leaders to siphon off hundreds of millions to put in their Swiss bank accounts, why not require rigorous e-government so that everything can be tracked?

Initially this could be done at the municipal level. I've spoken with local leaders who claim they would be willing to implement such software in exchange for aid. A modest requirement could gradually force many such municipalities to follow suit; within a few years, it could become a requirement for aid that local governments implement an e-government system. Gradually this requirement could be applied to larger and larger units of government, and ultimately nations.

Finally, a word about blockchain technologies and bitcoin: first, there have been initiatives to use blockchain to document land titles. Without claiming that it is a magical solution, transparent public ledgers that cannot be altered without a record of such alteration is certainly a solution worth exploring in nations with notoriously bad recordkeeping systems and pervasive corruption.

Second, bitcoin is invaluable in nations with significant inflation and currency controls that prevent citizens from bringing capital in or out. In order for entrepreneurs to create prosperity in Africa, they need the freedom to deploy their choice of currency and to move capital freely. In many African nations, there are sharp restrictions on capital flows. But businesses often need to shift capital from one use to another quickly and frictionlessly. Many in the West have come to associate bitcoin with speculation, especially after the spectacular collapse of crypto exchange FTX. They are unaware of what it is like to live in a nation with weak financial institutions and, in many cases, chronically high inflation rates. Bitcoin is also a path to liberation from the CFA, a French-controlled currency that is currently used by fifteen nations and 180 million-plus people.

STARTUP CITIES.

"Startup Cities," also known as "Charter Cities," are part of a program that recognizes that prosperity is the natural result of access to what we call the "entrepreneurial toolkit." In that kit you'll find three essential tools: property rights, the rule of law, and freedom. In the course of the last century, every nation that has provided its citizens with access to these tools has become prosperous.

Ideally, governments would reform their policies to improve their business environments. Occasionally this actually happens—in Rwanda, President Paul Kagame explicitly models his reforms on those of Lee Kuan Yew, who brought prosperity to Singapore. As a consequence, in recent years, Rwanda has frequently been named a top performer on the Doing Business index. Rwanda has also been among the fastest-growing nations in Africa, despite being landlocked with few mineral resources. Rwanda also switched from Francophone to Anglophone, both in language and law. Michael Fairbanks, an American entrepreneur, has been advising Kagame and building relationships with US investors.

But more often, nations are stuck in a state of either socialism, which is hopeless, or crony capitalism, which tends to be slightly better but is still not conducive to true prosperity.

Hernando de Soto, who in 2002 was a finalist for the Nobel Prize in Economics, once said that when the United States or another nation signs a free-trade agreement with most nations, they are only signing the agreement with the top 10 percent of the population of their new partner because that's the approximate percentage of those who have access to secure property rights.

But there is another approach, one that has the advantage of not requiring clumsy, lumbering ships of state to correct their course: Special Economic Zones (SEZs), which we also identify under the rubric of Startup Cities. They provide for greater economic activity within the zone, which then leads to greater economic freedom nationwide, and finally to greater prosperity nationwide. Do they work? Look at South Korea, China, India, Mexico, Mauritius, and Ireland for examples of the spectacular success that can result.

Let me answer your first question: why would the central governments allow such freedom to be planted in their otherwise top-down systems? Bob Haywood, former executive director of the World Economic Processing Zones Association, provides some history, saying that typically zones are supported not by the central oligarchs, whose wealth depends on exclusive control of airports, banks, media, etc., but rather by those in the outer circle of oligarchy: the younger sons, cousins, in-laws, etc. They are close enough to have the ear of the oligarch but don't typically have direct access to the levers of wealth and power. They make the case that if, for example, they are given an export processing zone that doesn't compete with local businesses, they can make money without undermining the special privileges of the elites.

Once these zones begin to succeed—typically through lower taxes and lesser regulation—the oligarchs themselves become interested, and they invest in and expand the zones. A business class arises that is much larger than what was originally envisioned, and in the process, a wealthy and powerful voice for greater economic freedom grows nationwide.

In 2001, Dubai piloted the next generation of zones when it created the Dubai International Financial Centre (DIFC). Earlier zones had primarily consisted of reduced taxes and regulations but were still embedded in the standard UAE Sharia law legal system. But if one looks at the world's top financial centers— New York, London, Singapore, Hong Kong, Chicago, Sydney— they all use a version of British common law. The DIFC was designed so that a common law legal system would apply on all commercial transactions within the 110 acres of the zone.

With this new system in place, Dubai rapidly skyrocketed to become a top global financial center, breaking the top twenty in its first decade and the top ten less than twenty years after launch. This was a stunning achievement—so stunning, in fact, that a few years ago, Abu Dhabi copied the entire design, including staffing it with reputable international experts in British common law. In 2022, Dubai announced that they would be helping Colombia create a common law zone.

In 2009, Honduras passed legislation thanks to Octavio Sánchez, the chief of staff of President Lobo. Sánchez had been envisioning such a zone for nearly a decade, along with his American consultant, Mark Klugmann. I'm proud to say my husband, Michael, was an essential player in getting the new zone in place. While providing Socratic Educational Consulting for Universidad Francisco Marroquín (UFM) in Guatemala, he became close to Giancarlo Ibargüen, the school's president at the time. "Gianca" had also envisioned such zones, and thus when news came that Honduras was working toward installing zones with their own legal systems, Gianca introduced Michael to key players. Michael gathered a team and ultimately signed the first MOU with the government of Honduras to develop the zone.

The story of its passage is long and tortured and includes many memorable fights, including the rejection of the first proposed plan by the Honduran Supreme Court. That plan was put forth by Paul Romer, an American economist and Nobel Prize winner. Included in his plan was the suggestion that another country should control the legal system within the zone, a clear violation of national sovereignty and indeed a slap in the face to the Hondurans. Subsequent legislation was revised to provide governance in the zone as an extension of municipal autonomy—thus, "Startup Cities."

In May 2020, Prospera, a Zone for Economic Development and Employment (ZEDE) was launched on the island of Roatan off the coast of Honduras. Investment and talent are streaming in, which will hopefully lead to dramatic prosperity similar to that seen in Dubai, Hong Kong, and Singapore.

In recent years, the global movement to promote these jurisdictions has exploded. There are currently several prospective projects in Africa, though none is based on legislation that provides as much autonomy as the Honduran ZEDE.

As in Dubai and Abu Dhabi, ZEDE provides a common law legal system with an independent commercial law and regulatory system. That is what the Cheetah Alliance will pursue for Africa. There are promising starts already launched in Africa, with Enyimba Economic City in Nigeria winning first place globally in the Charter Cities Institute's business plan competition in 2019. Other promising possibilities include Nkwashi, Zambia; Talent City, Nigeria; and possibly Akon City, Senegal (although it is not yet clear if Akon City will provide significant regulatory streamlining). The Charter Cities Institute, a nonprofit organization, has agreements in the works in half a dozen other African countries to develop similar projects. This movement has gotten attention in *Wired magazine, The Financial Times, African Business, and fDi Intelligence. It is happening.*

As you may have noticed, neither e-government nor Startup Cities requires Pan-African cooperation—or anything like it. I can tell you from experience that's a good thing. If we can get broader cooperation across the continent, that is great. I'm excited about the African Continental Free Trade Area (AfCTA), but I'm not holding my breath to wait for it to be fully implemented, and some of the details make me cringe.

◇◇◇◇◇◇◇◇◇◇◇◇◇◇◇◇◇

The huge ethnic discrepancies are another reason to focus on creating pockets of excellence rather than redrawing national borders. We should reestablish and celebrate the distinctions that our hundreds of tribes and ethnicities can bring to the table. I would love to begin in Senegal because that's my home. But if there is a better place, I will go there.

As with anything, having buy-in from everyone is better. But we don't need that. Michael told me long ago that when you're facing a daunting problem affecting many, many people, you should instead focus on creating one island of excellence, no matter how small. Everyone else will take notice.

What's going on over there? How did they do that? When people start asking those questions, that is the point when they will be ready to listen. Human beings are human beings. You inspire them with a dream.

This is the vision: in five years, we'll have five to ten Startup Cities across Africa, new jurisdictions with world-class law and governance and cutting-edge education, attracting our best and brightest entrepreneurs to create new companies, new jobs, new innovations, and new wealth! Then in ten years, we'll have thirty to forty such cities going, and in forty years, hundreds, now seeded with dozens of successful African-owned and created multinational corporations in new industries and hundreds of smaller African companies supplying them with world-class goods and services.

This kind of aggressive acceleration of progress is how Africa becomes one of the leading regions for entrepreneurship, innovation, and wealth creation on Earth. I see a future in which Wakanda fantasies are outpaced by reality in the decades to come.

◇◇◇◇◇◇◇◇◇◇◇◇◇◇

There is another question that's haunted me for years: *what can I do to help?*

Many years ago, I did not know what to say. Today, I do.

Here's what you can do to make Africa's future a prosperous one:

1. **Support African entrepreneurs and businesses:** Whether you're a consumer, an investor, or a donor, you can make a difference by supporting African entrepreneurs and businesses. If you want to learn about or buy products and services from African-owned companies or you're interested in investing in Africa, just visit CheetahGeneration.com. You can also sign up for my newsletter at MagatteWade.com, where I share resources and recommendations.

2. **Advocate for Startup Cities:** When conversations about Africa come up in your social circles, you now have a new concept to talk about: Startup Cities. You can also write to your elected officials, join advocacy groups, and participate in public discussions about the need for world-class business environments in Africa to unleash entrepreneurship and innovation.

3. **Join the movement:** Above all, please stay connected to those who are passionate about creating positive change in Africa. Attend conferences. Join trips to Africa. Read books. Share articles, and talk with like-minded individuals. My community—the members of the Cheetah Generation—is ready to welcome you at CheetahGeneration.com.

Thank you for taking the time to read my story and for joining me on this journey. I invite you to continue along with me as we create this new world together. Come join us in making it happen! There is room for everyone!

Because when Africa finally achieves prosperity, it will unlock a future so bright we can hardly imagine it.

That, my friend, is a future worth fighting for.

POSTSCRIPT: IBOU

◇◇◇◇◇◇◇◇◇◇◇◇◇◇◇

A FTER WRITING MOST OF THIS MANUSCRIPT IN 2020, I returned to Senegal in April 2021 after being away for well over a year due to COVID-19. It was the longest I had been away since I began Adina.

I spent the first week back home mostly catching up with Ibou and his family. It was Ramadan, so we would break the fast joyfully every evening and then talk and laugh long into the night. It was a wonderful welcome home.

About a week in, Ibou came down with an infection. After a couple of days, I took him to the hospital in Mékhé for treatment. A nurse gave him some antibiotics and other pills and claimed he would get better soon.

That evening, he entered a delirious state, semiconscious, talking incoherently and stumbling and falling when he got up to go to the bathroom. I became very concerned.

Late in the evening, he finally agreed to let me take him to a hospital in a nearby town, some forty-five minutes away. It was a Friday night. When we pulled up at the emergency entrance, no one came out to meet us. The staff stood at the door and watched as we pulled him out of the car. He was a big, heavy, delirious man, and there were no healthcare workers to help us.

When we got inside, the doctor on staff didn't have any suggestions except that maybe he should get a brain scan in case he was having a stroke. They told me the only CT scanner operating at that hour was in Dakar, another hour and a half away. I asked if they could take him there in the ambulance. They said they didn't know where the ambulance was. It had gone to Dakar and might be back in a few hours, or maybe not until morning. I was worried, furious, and anxious, trying to make a decision. That was when one of the nurses got closer to me and whispered, "Do you have a car?"

"Yes," I replied.

She said, "I suggest you use your own car and go. Drive slow. God is good, and by his grace, you will get there. Go. Now."

So my driver and I got him back into the car on our own. At this point he was holding his head painfully as we bumped over the rough highway. I sat in the back, cradling his head and trying to protect him from the pain as the car bounced along.

Eventually we got to the emergency room of the hospital. They did a scan and saw nothing. But he was admitted to the ER. Unfortunately, I was not allowed to see him. It was very difficult to get any information out of them. The ER staff were again listless and passive. I went back home to get a few hours of sleep and check on the kids and then came back again on Saturday. His sodium levels were dangerously low, so they put him on an IV. I bribed one of the desk staff so they would let me see him (due to COVID-19 restrictions, patients were not allowed visits). He was in a room with a window, and they took me outside his window and opened it so I could talk with him. He was weak and unhappy to be in the hospital, but at least he could talk, and he wasn't delirious anymore.

By Sunday night, he seemed to be better. He really wanted to go back home to be with his children and sleep in his own bed. I took him back to Mékhé. He was still in the bloody, dirty clothes that I had brought him in on Friday night. They had not changed him or bathed him—nothing.

When I use the word "hospital" in the comfortable countries of the West, most would usually envision a clean, sanitary space. But this particular ER was not so much. You really have no idea what I'm talking about here. You also expect professional, knowledgeable, and compassionate staff, but I was mostly meeting with uncaring staff who seemed to have little interest in helping me or Ibou and no interest in giving me much information. They were just moving around listlessly. Maybe they were just exhausted, especially in those times of COVID-19, with not enough resources. But it made for a horrible experience for Ibou and me.

Back in Mékhé, he seemed to be better for a few days. Then he became delirious again, almost certainly due to low sodium levels. Because he was too weak to return to Dakar, we had to turn to the nearby hospital in Mékhé. At least the children and I could visit him there. The hospital sent an "ambulance" to pick him up this time.

At least the hospital staff in the small town of Mékhé allowed us to feed him, clean him, and care for him. Simply in terms of human dignity, that struck me as better than leaving him at the mercy of the ER staff in Dakar. They put him back on a sodium IV, and he again seemed to be getting better.

On Friday, his family came to see him. They decided he should be moved back to a hospital in Dakar. They had the traditional respect for hospitals in the capital. How could I blame them? I had also felt that way until I actually saw one up close myself. I tried to argue, but they had the legal rights, and their opinion could not be swayed.

I went home that night and cried and cried for fear that this was his death sentence.

Once he was in the hospital in Dakar, I again had a hard time getting any information about him. Fortunately, the nurse I had previously bribed gave me an update: he was unconscious but seemed stable. The next day, however, we heard from the doctor supervising him that he was in critical condition. We tried to get vital signs, but they would tell us nothing more.

Monday he again seemed better.

Tuesday morning his brother called to let me know that he had died.

That afternoon we buried him.

We don't refrigerate or embalm our dead in Senegal. We bury them soon after death.

People die all the time in Senegal. This just happened to be one of the most important people in my life. I had spent the previous ten days fighting to get care for him, without any good information, in a system that none of you would find acceptable for anyone you cared about.

I drove down with his oldest son to the funeral. We didn't tell the younger children because we couldn't take them all, and I didn't want to leave them alone with the horrible news. At the viewing service, Ibou was covered in white cloth, as is our custom. I touched him one last time before they proceeded to finish covering his face and feet. They had to carry me out of there. I was suffocating, screaming, and crying uncontrollably, all at the same time.

When I got back to Mékhé that evening, I had to do one of the hardest things I have ever done since burying my first husband. I paused before entering his home, in dread of what was coming.

When I opened the door, the children rushed at me, big-eyed, enthusiastically asking, "Is our daddy better?"

I miss Ibou terrifically. This book is dedicated to his memory.

ACKNOWLEDGMENTS

◇◇◇◇◇◇◇◇◇◇◇◇◇

PORTIONS OF THIS BOOK are drawn from materials I created earlier, including interviews and speeches. These texts were then revised to suit the format of this book. I appreciate the cooperation of those who first published my words in print, video, or podcast, including the Foundation for Economic Education, TED, John Stossel, the Acton Institute (producers of Poverty, Inc.), and Valerie Hinkle and Jared H. H-Marshall, who created Made in Mékhé. A special thank you to Stephen Hicks, PhD, for his interview published in Kaizen, the newsletter for the Center for Ethics and Entrepreneurship at Rockford College.

Thank you to Atlas Network, including Brad Lips, Linda Whetstone (RIP 1942-2021), and all the Atlas Network partners and donors for supporting our work together at the Center for African Prosperity. My thanks also to Inge Herbert and the Friedrich Naumann Foundation for their generous support.

The chapter titles are from Dr. Richard Shawyer's (dit Musaa Sarr) Wisdom of the Wolof Sages, a marvelous collection he has made available on the internet.

I also want to thank Duggan Flanakin and Mark St. J. Couhig for their research and editorial advice, as well as Caleb Capoccia for his support with research.

Thank you to my beloved Professor George Ayittey (RIP 1945-2022) for his moral and intellectual integrity in researching and documenting the truth about free enterprise in pre-colonial Africa—especially when it was not a popular message. George, you opened my mind and heart in ways unimaginable. You are deserving of a Nobel Prize, and I trust history will remember your name.

Thank you to my dear friends who have supported me along this journey, including Ibrahima N'Dour, Gerry Ohrstrom, Frayda and Ken Levy, Vidar Jorgensen, John Mackey, Michaella Rugwizangoga, Chris Rufer, Bob Chitester (1937-2012), Sylvie Légère, Anne Davidson, Andreas Widmer, Gonzalo Schwarz, Father Sirico, Mark Weber, Michael Matheson Miller, Carol and Eldon Wentz, Delilah Rothenberg, George Scharffenberger, Sophie Ravel, Larry Bailey, Maya Ravel-Bailey, Alison Davis, Jim and Maureen Tusty, Bill Pearson and family, Sean Malone, Richard Lorenc, Larry Reed, Gabriel and Karen Calzada, Lawson and Cynthia Bader, Matt and Terri Kibbe, and so many more. You have all welcomed me with open arms, always respected me and my mind, and showed me your support in the most undeniable ways.

And a very special thank you to Emmanuel Marchand, his mother Marie-Claude Leboeuf and her entire family.

A unique, special and infinite gratitude for my wonderful grandmother, Mame Arame Ngom.

Last, but not least, I want to thank my Beloved M, Michael Strong.

Loving is not looking at one another, it's looking together in the same direction.
—Antoine de Saint-Exupéry

Most people think that love is simply about the romance of being together. For me it is about serving a higher purpose together. The love between Michael and me is undeniable and all powerful. We use it to serve a purpose greater than ourselves: the eradication of global poverty by helping those in currently impoverished nations to rise so they, too, can live prosperous, happy, healthy, and productive lives. So no, we are not looking at each other. Instead, we hold each other tightly, look in the same direction, and advance courageously and confidently as we pave the way toward our vision of a better world.

Printed in Great Britain
by Amazon